IN SEARCH OF
CHEDDAR MAN

Larry Barham

Philip Priestley & Adrian Targett

Foreword by Mick Aston

TEMPUS

Dedication (from Larry Barham)

To my parents and to Mary for their unfailing support
in this and so much more

Dedication (from Adrian Targett)

To my mother Hilda Targett 1922-1997
for whom family always came first

First published 1999

Published by:
Tempus Publishing Limited
The Mill, Brimscombe Port
Stroud, Gloucestershire, GL5 2QG

Typesetting and origination by Tempus Publishing Ltd.
Printed and bound in Great Britain.

British Library Cataloguing in Publication Data.

A catalogue record for this book is available from the British Library.

ISBN 07524 1401 1

Contents

Acknowledgements

The following people and organisations have helped with ideas, information, encouragement, criticism and images for illustration: Andy Currant, Chris Stringer, Peter Andrews, Stephen-Aldhouse Green, Lars Larsson, Mary Earnshaw, Sue Giles (Bristol City Museum), NERC Ancient Biomolecules Initiative, Bob Smart (Cheddar Showcaves), Wookey Caves, Simon Lumkin (Pioneer Group), Kate Robson-Brown, Jodie Lewis, David Mullin, Stuart Prior, and Samantha Eyre. A debt of gratitude is owed to Mick Aston and Philip Priestley for involving me in the project from the start, to Stephen Aldhouse-Green for a critical reading of the text (I take full responsibility for *Bunny fluffy*) and to Sue Grice for her lively artwork and patience.

Larry Barham

Thanks are also due to: Melanie Caple, Allie Davies, Daphne Ireland, Harvey Lilley, Janet & Rodney Mears, Janet Nearn, Karen Olds, Chris Richardson, Bob Smart, Charles Targett, Katie Targett and Kate West.

Philip Priestley & Adrian Targett

The cover photograph, of Adrian Targett and his ancestor, was taken by Matthew Priestley.

Foreword

By Professor Mick Aston

When I was approached by Philip Priestley and Harvey Lilley to make a series of six landscape archaeology programmes for HTV, I was very pleased. I have always believed in making archaeology accessible to the public so that the enthusiasm and passionate interest for the subject can be conveyed to everyone else. Television is the most effective way of doing this. In each of my jobs — museum archaeologist, County archaeologist, tutor in local studies at Oxford University and until recently Staff Tutor in Archaeology at the University of Bristol — my aim has been to make the subject available to as many people as possible.

With the Time Team programmes for Channel 4 we have been able to do this, I believe, on a grand scale. After 40+ programmes we regularly get audiences of 3-4 million — and I am told that 13 million (or a quarter of the population) has watched at least part of a programme. Tony Robinson, a good friend of mine, presents these programmes and does a super job of being the 'person in the street' as well as professionally doing all the 'pieces to camera'.

I was attracted to working on a local HTV series for several reasons. I much admired other work that Chris Chapman (Exmoor, Quantocks, and the Levels series) and other members of the production company had done. I also wanted to do my own 'pieces to camera' — I now realise of course how difficult they are and how good at it Tony is! But mainly I wanted to look at some local sites and landscapes that excite and interest me.

I knew I would have no problem in thinking of venues. I have worked in and on the counties of Somerset (particularly), Avon (as was), Gloucester-shire and Wiltshire for nearly 20 years and I knew there were loads of places where interesting programmes could be made. The difficulty would be deciding on the first six — though not a problem if we could make more and more batches of sixes later on!

We covered Low Ham, Deserted Villages (on the Cotswolds), Medieval New Towns, the Severn Estuary, Avebury and, of course, Cheddar. My idea for this programme was that people had lived at Cheddar for nearly 15,000 years. I find it exciting that a place has been so continuously occupied for so long — few places can claim such continuity. Little did I realise the implications of that idea at the time!

This splendid book covers the extraordinary story which developed from that one programme, from the viewpoints of the producer Philip Priestley, who had the courage to go for the idea and stick with it, of Larry Barham one

Professor Mick Aston (photo: Matthew Priestley)

of the specialists of this period and a colleague of mine at the University of Bristol, and of Adrian Targett the schoolmaster who unwittingly was propelled into world celebrity status as a result of the DNA testing. Together they give us a fascinating picture of high-profile archaeology in the media world of today, while explaining the relevance of such studies — we are *all* involved in the common ancestry of our own species *homo sapiens*.

Larry Barham has written all the main chapters of In Search of Cheddar Man. *Philip Priestley has written sections that tell the unfolding story of the television programme that led to the discovery of Cheddar Man's living descendant. And Adrian Targett has written signed pieces about the experience of sudden fame and about his female ancestors as far back as he can trace them.*

1 The journey to Cheddar

How it all began — the discovery of Cheddar Man

The dust from the blast had cleared and a team of workmen armed with picks and shovels began shifting the rubble. Broken bones appeared and they were human — Cheddar Man had been discovered. It was Christmas 1903 at Gough's Cave, a well-known tourist attraction on the south side of Cheddar Gorge in Somerset, England. The owners of the cave were making improvements to their site. A drain was needed to cure the problem of winter flooding, an almost annual act of nature that was bad for business. A narrow fissure to the left of the main entrance was targeted, the blasting began and the rest is history, or prehistory in the case of Cheddar Man.

Almost a century later, winter flooding is still a problem for the management of Gough's Cave and Cheddar Man has achieved lasting fame. Thanks to the modern sciences of dating and genetics he has acquired new celebrity as the 9,000-year-old ancestor of Adrian Targett, a local history teacher. Archaeologists are used to dealing with fragments of bone and stone and stains in the ground but to come face to face with a living ancestor is unsettling. It reminds us what archaeology is really about — human beings. But even this is not as simple as it sounds, human beings have come in many different shapes and sizes over millions of years; some of them would be unrecognisable to us as relatives today. The range of early humans, that is members of our genus *Homo*, includes at least six different forms or species, all now extinct.

Today we are the only species of human on the planet, and we proudly call ourselves *Homo sapiens* or 'wise man'. Being alone on the planet is apparently something new for humans. Palaeoanthropologists — scientists who study the evolution of humans by comparing bones, genes and artefacts — tell us that until very recently — 30,000 years ago is yesterday — we shared the earth with at least one other species of *Homo* called *Homo neanderthalensis* or simply Neanderthal. The fact that we are the sole representatives of a long lineage of human ancestors is telling us something important. *Homo sapiens* has successfully colonised all the continents, except Antarctica (for the time being), has planted a flag on the moon and sent probes beyond the solar system. We are restless. But what happened to our partners, the Neanderthals? Why did they not share that Apollo 11 ride to the moon?

Archaeology tackles big issues, it asks what makes us human and how we came to live and behave the way we do today. That is the broad theme of this book. Cheddar Man will lead us on a journey through time to trace the origin

1   *The patchwork landscape of the Somerset Levels from the Mendip hills.*

of 'wise man' via a distant ancestor, *Homo erectus*. Our wanderlust began with this now extinct species, the first human to leave Africa and settle in Asia and Europe. *Homo erectus* was also the ancestor of Neanderthals and the fate of *Homo neanderthalensis* is very much part of Cheddar Man's story. His direct ancestors — and they were ours too — played an active role in this evolutionary drama.

The final stage of the journey witnesses the transformation of Cheddar Man's descendants from hunters and gatherers to farmers. Without farming you would not be reading this book, driving a car or doing most of the things we take for granted. Farming changed us as a species and changed the way we see the world around us. The genetic link between Cheddar Man and Adrian Targett is a big clue to how this change came about. While the fast moving science of genetics plays a starring role in this story, in the end it is the painstaking study of the stones and bones of prehistory — and the people who left them behind them — which allows us to see how humans evolved.

Before Cheddar Man — setting the scene

On the Mendip hills high above Gough's Cave the view to the south takes in a landscape of distant hills, the flat patchwork fields of the Somerset Levels and a tongue of sea that is the Bristol Channel (**1**). Forget, for a moment, the world of motorways, industry and tourism. With a bit of imagination you can see the landscape Cheddar Man saw some 9,000 years ago. The hills are covered with birch, pine and hazel forest which spreads down to the valley below to join the banks of a smoothly flowing river. The sluggish managed waterways of the Levels today are a thing of the future and the sea is just a

8

glimmer in the far distance. Imagining that is easy, similar landscapes exist in Britain and northern Europe today. More challenging to the imagination is the landscape of the Mendips during the last ice age, not only colder and treeless but filled with unfamiliar animals such as the mammoth, woolly rhinoceros and spotted hyaena.

Twelve thousand years ago Cheddar Man's ancestors lived in this landscape. They were human like us and skilled hunter-gatherers who probably had a life rich in ritual. These ice age forebears arrived in Britain over 30,000 years ago but they were not the first people to live on Mendip. Another human species, Neanderthals (*Homo neanderthalensis*), had made this area their home as long ago as 60,000 BP (BP is the scientific convention for years 'before present') and may have been still living here when *Homo sapiens* arrived. To imagine the world of Neanderthals is an even greater challenge. Not only did they live in ice age landscapes, but Neanderthals themselves were different from us both in the way they lived and in the way they looked. These two different species were both human, but were they both related, did they share common roots? This is important to our understanding of Cheddar Man and his world — and his relationship to ours.

What is a species?

To follow the story of our human ancestors it is important to understand what a species is, how species evolve and why they die out. This is complicated in the prehistoric world in which Cheddar Man lived. We depend on fragments of information which we have to piece together carefully. Identifying a species is difficult where evidence is scarce, recognising when one species evolves into another is even more difficult when change is slow and the fossil record is piecemeal. Complete skeletons, like that of Cheddar Man, are the exception. Usually, only the hardest and densest bones survive such as teeth, jaws, bits of the skull, hip and thigh. The uneven preservation of human remains is one problem. Another, and even more taxing problem, is defining just what makes a fossil species. How do we decide if a human who lived one million or just nine thousand years ago was really a different species from ourselves?

Most biologists agree that a **species** is a community of organisms in which individuals resemble each other because they interbreed among themselves, and do not breed successfully with any other kinds of organisms. Members of a living species, by definition, have offspring which can also produce offspring. So, for example, female rabbits of a species we will call *Bunny fluffy* give birth only to *Bunny fluffy* bunnies and so on. We know what *Bunny fluffy* rabbits look like and, assuming all member of this species look more or less alike, then we can assign individual rabbits to this species by appearance. Judging by appearance can save a lot of time and bother, watching and waiting for individuals to reproduce. But appearances can be deceptive. *Bunny fluffies* might differ in size, colour, shape of nose, or the like, especially if they live in different environments, but still be the same species. To be more certain, biologists can compare DNA — the genetic material which is the building

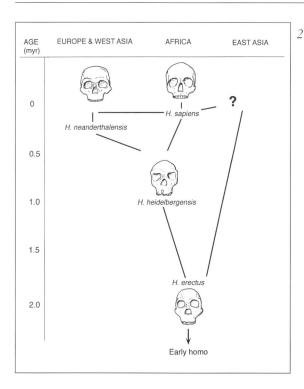

2   An evolutionary tree showing an Out of Africa version of the origin of Homo sapiens. *In this diagram, living humans and Neanderthals (*Homo neanderthalensis*) are descendants of* Homo heidelbergensis *which evolved from* Homo erectus. *Neanderthals are an extinct branch of the family tree, replaced by us (*Homo sapiens*) (after Stringer & Mckie 1996).*

block of life — between individuals to see how closely they are related, although even comparing genes is not foolproof. Sometimes two populations of individuals which look and act like different species might in fact be genetically similar. Or, unrelated species can sometimes look alike because they evolved in similar environments like deserts, rain forests or caves. Working with the living is not as easy as it looks.

How then do we recognise fossil human species and their ancestry when all we have are fragmentary bones? Palaeoanthropologists assume that fossils which are similar in details of skeletal anatomy *probably* belong to the same species especially if they are from a similar environment and roughly the same time. Some features of the skeleton are more important than others for defining a fossil species, especially those which reflect how it made a living. Eating, fighting, fleeing, mating and communicating are all basic behaviours which leave evolutionary traces on the skeleton. These traces can be measured and comparisons made between fossils to determine which clusters of traits best define a particular species. To build an evolutionary tree or **phylogeny** from fossils, palaeoanthropologists must first decide which traits — and the behaviours they reflect — are shared and which are new (**2**). As a rule of thumb, species which shared a recent ancestor will be more similar than species which separated long ago.

Phylogenetic analysis is rarely this straightforward. Palaeoanthropologists often disagree on which skeletal features define a species, on how much they differ *within* a species and on how much they can change before declaring a new species. It is not a simple job and sometimes personal pride gets in the way. Palaeoanthropologists are human after all and do not give up their dearly held theories without a fight. The discovery of DNA in the teeth of Cheddar Man is so exciting because of these difficulties — it is a genuine breakthrough in reconstructing the ancestry of Europeans.

Reconstructing our ancestry involves more than comparing bumps on bones. It is also about ways of behaving. Species have different ways of behaving or responding to the challenges of the world around them. To understand how they behaved we need to know what stresses they faced, such as climate, availability of water, food, shelter, raw materials for tools and threats from other animals — including other humans. This is the archaeological record. Skeletons tell a partial story of people responding to their surroundings. The archaeological record tells another. Together they give us the clues to piece together the jigsaw of human evolution.

Where did we come from, where did Neanderthals go?

Neanderthals are an important part of Cheddar Man's story, but were they our ancestors or did we, *Homo sapiens*, evolve somewhere else and from another ancestor? The fate of Neanderthals divides archaeologist and palaeoanthropologists into competing tribes. The debate boils down to a simple question: did modern humans evolve in Africa fairly recently — about 200,000 years ago — and then spread across the Old World, replacing other human species in Asia and Europe, or did we evolve as a single species across the Old World over more than a million years? This is the 'Out of Africa' debate which started in earnest in the late 1980s.

Chris Stringer and Peter Andrews of the Natural History Museum, London, were the first to combine fossil and new genetic evidence to argue that Neanderthals were not our ancestors. They compared fossils from Africa, the Middle East and Europe and concluded that modern humans evolved in Africa and did so very recently by the time scale of evolution. New scientific dating techniques (see Appendix) had made it possible for the first time to determine the age of fossils older than 40,000 years, which is the limit of the accuracy of radiocarbon dating. The new dates showed that Neanderthals and modern humans lived in the Middle East at the same time. It seemed unlikely that Neanderthals were our ancestors.

Stringer and Andrews published their argument in 1988 which included the results of genetic analyses from the laboratory of Alan Wilson at the University of California, Berkeley. Wilson and his colleagues provided independent support for a recent African genesis. Their analysis of DNA taken from blood samples of living humans led them to the conclusion that all humans are genetically very similar, and that as a species we are very young with African roots. This was dubbed the 'African Eve' theory by the media in the frenzy which followed.

Race is a sensitive concept for anthropologists especially in this century when it has been so abused to justify mistreatment and murder. An African Eve challenges our ideas about the origin of human races. It says that the physical differences we see between peoples today evolved only recently —

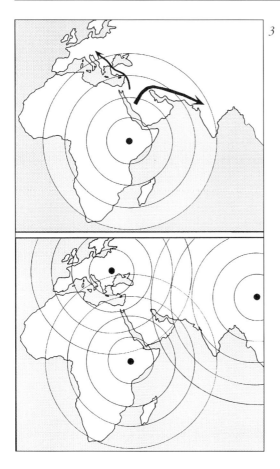

3   *In the Out of Africa model of modern human origins (top)* Homo sapiens *evolved in Africa about 200,000 years ago and spread into Asia and later into Europe, replacing indigenous populations. In the Multiregional model (bottom), humans evolved as a single species at the same time in Africa, Asia and Europe because they were connected by intricate networks of alliances along which people, and their genes, moved.*

after modern humans had spread across the Old World — and that beneath the skin we are all Africans.

The alternative theory is that modern humans evolved across the Old World over a long period of time and it is called the **multiregional hypothesis**. It says races are ancient adaptations to the regions where they are found today. *Homo sapiens* evolved together in Africa, Asia and Europe, connected by a vast network of mates, and the genes they carried, being exchanged between hunter-gatherer camps (**3**). This way all the major evolutionary changes which go to make up modern humans would be evenly distributed but the smaller regional differences, or races, would be left to develop. Neanderthals were simply the European version of us and should be labelled as *Homo sapiens neanderthalensis* to emphasise their close link to living humans.

These are two very different explanations for the evolutionary process which produced us and Cheddar Man, which is why Neanderthals are so important. Their fate is a test of the two theories. If they were our close kin then the multiregional theory makes sense, but if they were not our ancestors than the theory of an African origin wins, at least in Europe. To test this theory, palaeoanthropologists compare the evidence of bones, artefacts and

DNA in the search for similarities and differences. Deciding which theory best fits the evidence or which bits of evidence are the most significant is the stuff of controversy. It depends on our understanding of the workings of evolution and this varies between scientists.

What was the weather like?

Stones and bones are the archaeological evidence of human evolution, but to understand the forces that shaped us as a species we must consider the environment in its broadest sense and in particular climate change.

Climate can affect where we live and how we earn our living no less today than it did millions of years ago. We are living at a time when scientists are hotly debating the likelihood of global warming — and, even more contentiously, its possible causes. For our human ancestors there was no such luxury of prediction, they had to live with the vagaries of climate and all that meant in terms of the availability of food sources and shelter, or move on to somewhere more hospitable. The climate also affected their access to habitable territory, whether it was a rising sea drowning land bridges, or glaciers and deserts posing formidable barriers.

The glacial clock

The most enduring environmental challenge faced by the earliest humans and by the later ancestors of Cheddar Man was the fluctuating climate of the many ice ages. Over the past two million years the earth has experienced at least 63 major fluctuations in climate from cold to warm conditions. The old idea of a single Ice Age has been replaced by the regular ticking of a global climatic clock which affects all life. The cycle of alternating cold or **glacials** periods with warm **interglacials** was underway by 2.4 million years ago. For most of this period, the length and intensity of the glacials and interglacials has varied but starting about 700,000 years ago the intervals of cold became longer. The climatic clock has been ticking away in the background of human evolution with a regular beat of about 100,000 years per glacial cycle. The cycle involves a relatively brief interglacial of about 10,000-20,000 years duration and a glacial phase about 60,000-80,000 years long (**4**).

Glacial periods are not uniformly cold from the start to finish. Temperatures gradually drop over thousands of years leading to a period of maximum cold followed by a rapid warming. Shorter intervals of warm conditions — on the order of 500-2,000 years long — often punctuate glacial periods. These are known as **interstadials**. Likewise, the warm interglacials are sometimes interrupted by short cold pulses known as **stadials**.

The many flip-flops in climate challenged human resilience and ingenuity, especially the rapid shifts from glacial to interglacial conditions. Recent climatic evidence from cores drilled into the ice cap of Greenland reveals a remarkable record of yearly changes in temperature spanning the last 130,000 years. The cores show that the global warming that brings a glacial period to an end can take place in a human lifetime. Fortunately for us, the shift from

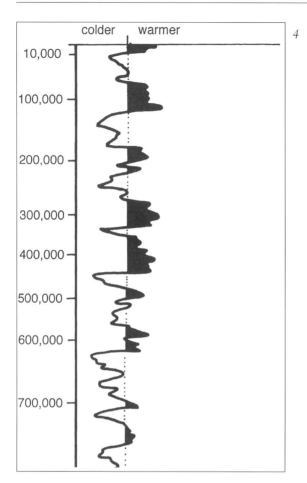

4   *The rhythmic cycle of climate change glacial (white) to interglacial (black) periods during the past 700,000 years.*

warm interglacial conditions like those we enjoy today is much more gradual, on the order of a few thousand years. Cooling down takes longer than warming up.

The explanation for the increasing regularity of glacial cycles is complex and involves changes in the earth's orbit around the sun and a host of geological, biological and chemical reactions which take place on earth. The details are not important to this story, but what is significant is the effect of longer glacial periods on the early human settlement of Europe. The alternating cycle of glacials and interglacials profoundly alters the distribution of plants, animals and humans. During glacial periods in Europe, ice sheets form in the Alps, Scandinavia and Siberia with the ice sheets of highland Britain merging at times with the Scandinavian ice to cover much of northern Europe (**5**). The world sea level drops by as much as 370 ft (120m) as sea water feeds the growing ice sheets. One effect of lowered sea level is the opening of new land bridges. Britain becomes part of mainland Europe as the North Sea and English Channel become dry land. Many of the islands of the Mediterranean become linked, like Malta to Sicily, and a land bridge between Tunisia and Italy may have emerged. The lowered sea level also changed the

14

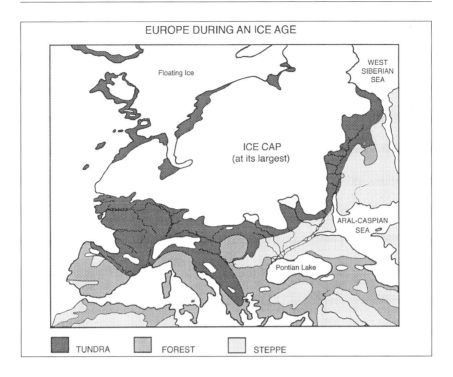

EUROPE DURING AN ICE AGE

WEST SIBERIAN SEA

Floating Ice

ICE CAP
(at its largest)

ARAL-CASPIAN SEA

Pontian Lake

TUNDRA   FOREST   STEPPE

5   *The distribution of ice sheets and vegetation across Europe during a typical glacial period. (after Goodes World Atlas 1978)*

courses of major rivers, such as the Thames and Severn.

Zones of plant and animal life were pushed far to the south of their current distribution. A cross-section through Europe during the last ice age (**6a**) shows a very different landscape from today. Conditions near the margins of the ice sheets were too cold and dry for life, creating a polar desert. Beyond the ice sheets the soil was a zone of permanently frozen soil which took in the Mendips (**6b**). An open steppe tundra landscape of short grasses and herbs spread from southern Ireland, across northern France and east into Germany, Poland and onwards into Siberia. This grassland supported large herds of grazing animals including woolly mammoth, reindeer, horse, bison and musk ox. Further south the open tundra graded into birch and dwarf birch forest. Across southern Europe around the Mediterranean the vegetation also reflected the cooler drier conditions with a mixture of steppe plants and patches of pine forest.

During interglacials Europe's climate would have been much like it is now, with modern coastlines and glaciers restricted to the Arctic and mountain ranges. Vegetation would recolonise former glacial areas in a well-known sequence beginning with trees and shrubs which could tolerate bare soils. Birch, pine and hazel would be some of the first colonists, followed by mixed forests of oak, elm and ash as soils improved. These mature deciduous forests would gradually include hornbeam, fir and spruce before soils and climate deteriorate and the vegetation returns to a birch, pine and spruce mix.

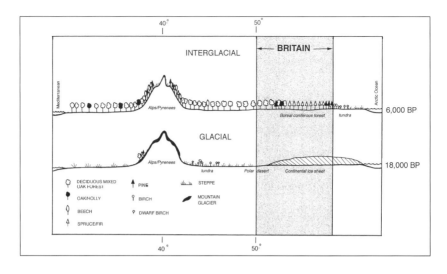

6a   *A cross-section of western Europe during an interglacial (top) and glacial period (bottom) showing the dramatic shifts in vegetation with climate. The position of Britain is shown in grey (not to scale) (after Van der Hammen et al 1971).*

This is a very general outline of glacial and interglacial changes in plant types which will vary in detail of species and distribution across Europe, but it gives a sense of the enormity of the changes which took place regularly during the past 700,000 years.

Climate change in Europe had a profound impact on human development, but those humans first emerged from Africa, where climate change played an equally important role in the evolutionary story. Environmental scientists now realise that the tropics experienced dramatic shifts in temperature and rainfall during the ice ages, going back at least 2.4 million years. In Africa, the shift from glacial to interglacial was from cool, dry conditions to warmer and wetter like today. The cool dry conditions of the glacials spurred the spread of deserts, especially the Sahara in the north and the Kalahari in the south (**7**). Deserts were the African equivalent of the European ice sheets. They isolated populations of animals and plants and created the conditions for new species to emerge and others to become extinct.

The rhythmic pulse of deserts spreading and shrinking with the ice ages was the background beat to human evolution from the very start. How early humans responded by way of technology, social organisation and beliefs is what really interests archaeologists. The past becomes for us a laboratory for observing and comparing the development of our ancestors' abilities to cope with change.

6b   The extent of ice and permafrost in Britain 18,000 years ago during the coldest phase of the last glacial cycle (after Goudie 1992).

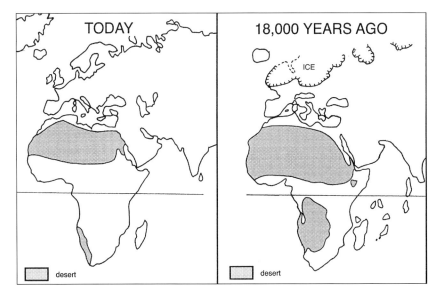

7   The expansion and contraction of deserts in Africa during interglacial (left) and glacial (right) periods (after Goudie 1992).

A TOSS-UP

In the beginning it was a toss-up — Avebury or Cheddar. Tom Archer of HTV had commissioned us to make a series of six programmes on archaeology. The HTV West region covers Bristol, and parts of Gloucestershire, Wiltshire, Somerset, and Dorset. The films were to be presented by Mick Aston, recently promoted professor at Bristol University and well known to millions as the enthusiast archaeologist of Channel Four's Time Team programme. We began talking with him in mid-1996. He suggested a dozen good stories in Somerset, Gloucestershire and Wiltshire and Harvey Lilley and I — trading as EPIK TV — were dividing them between ourselves so that we could direct three each. They were all interesting places with intriguing histories attached to them, but the two obvious plums in the list were Avebury and Cheddar. Avebury is a vast sacred landscape south of Swindon with a Bronze Age stone circle big enough to hold a village. An impressive stone avenue leads from the circle and about half a mile away there is the mighty man-made Silbury Hill — a chopped-off cone big enough to cover the whole of Stonehenge like a tea-cosy. Cheddar is the site of a spectacular series of Saxon royal palaces; has the famous Gorge, and two renowned and much visited showcaves. We both really fancied doing Avebury and couldn't decide. I finally said to Harvey that he could choose, and he chose Avebury.

I wasn't deeply disappointed to be doing Cheddar. I live on the edge of the Mendips about twelve miles from the top of the famous Gorge, and the high point of my week is to drive that way home, through the nondescript nineteenth century sprawl of the village, past the Lourdes-like trinket shops, and the messed-about Frank Lloyd-Wright-like facade of Gough's Cave, past the towering cliffs above the Horseshoe, winding upwards out of the canyon and onto the Mendip Plateau near Priddy. It is an awe-inspiring piece of scenery, un-English in its drama, and in the evening light, or at night with sheets of moonlight hung out to dry on the limestone crags, a place where ghosts might dwell, where mysteries might lurk. The biggest mystery of all is the whereabouts of the gigantic 'Chederhole' described by Henry of Huntingdon in the twelfth century as containing 'great spaces of land and streams' but long since lost.

One of the attractions of the Gorge is the presence at Gough's Cave of the skeleton known as Cheddar Man; or rather his facsimile. He was uncovered in 1903 and is reputed to be the most complete Stone Age skeleton ever excavated in the British Isles (8). I first saw him almost 50 years ago in a glass case by the front entrance to the cave. Even in those days he was not the real thing. But the copy was good enough to provoke disturbing feelings. A whole set of human bones put on show for people to stare at. Half a million visitors a year now come to Cheddar; more than a third of a million of them visit the caves. The display of ancestral remains is currently a hot issue in the politics of archaeology — a lot of it bound up with nationalisms and anti-colonialisms; but even were that not the case, a sense of unease still clings to the exhibition of unburied human beings. It seems disrespectful of the dead; even the long dead.

REMARKABLE DISCOVERY IN CHEDDAR CAVES.

Mr H. St. George Gray, the curator of the Taunton Museum, who was formerly assistant to the late General Pitt-Rivers, the celebrated archæologist, has just examined, at the request of the Somerset Archæological and Natural History Society, a remarkable human skeleton which has been discovered in Gough's Caves at Cheddar. The remains are believed by Mr Gray to be those of a cave-dweller who lived between the Paleolithic and the Neolithic ages. The skull is in many fragments, and encrusted in loam. The man had very prominent brows. The forehead is of the usual width, but, on the other hand, it is very receding. The lower jaw is powerfully formed, and far beyond the width of those of the present age. The skull is also very thick. The thickest part of the frontal bone is nine millimêtres, while the average of the present day is only seven millimêtres. The skeleton was found between two layers of stalagmite. The height of the man was 5 feet 3¾ inches. In the Stone age the average height of a man was only about 5 feet 3 inches or 5 feet 4 inches, and that of a woman 4 feet 11 inches. The shin bone is flat, which is never the case at the present day. Flint implements were found near the skeleton of the type used by cave men.

8   *The bones of Cheddar Man*

Besides all that, from a programme point of view, Cheddar is picturesque, not just in a static picture post-card sense, but filmically as well. So I was pleased to be doing a programme about it. Another good thing was that Mick Aston lives less than five miles from the bottom of the Gorge, and as a former archaeology officer for Somerset he knew everybody who had ever dug there, or done surveys, or who was working there at the moment. We made a list of candidates for inclusion in the programme. I didn't want the Gorge and the Caves to take up all the space — they were the most obvious sites, the most well-known, but it would be good to reveal other, less expected things. Mick greatly admired Philip Rahtz, his teacher and mentor at Birmingham University, and retired Professor Emeritus at the University of York. Philip had dug the site of the proposed comprehensive school in Cheddar in 1960-2. It was the biggest dig he ever did and it crowned his illustrious career, yielding up rows of post holes from six successive West Saxon Royal Palaces — huge wooden structures the size of cathedrals where the Kings of Wessex and then of England had held court. King Alfred himself ruled intermittently from here, may have written, and certainly practised the Laws of his own Code — a landmark in the development of English criminal law. He may even have burned the famous cakes somewhere on the nearby moors. After the excavation, the local authority architect decided to mark some of the palace post-holes with concrete caps in what became an un-enclosed quadrangle in front of the restored ruins of former Royal Chapel. To the horror of Philip Rahtz the school itself was then built on un-dug land, the possible resting place of untold other evidence of Saxon or even earlier occupation. To commemorate the finds, the school was re-named Kings of Wessex School.

I resolve to ring the school for permission to film Mick and Philip in the grounds. At the same time I was trying to solve another kind of problem.

One of the drawbacks of archaeology on television is that a lot of it is intrinsically boring — 'humps and bumps' as Mick calls them, disturbed ground features that might or might not conceal buried treasure. Landscape archaeology tries to make sense of what can be seen on the surface. Conservative archaeology also prefers a non-intrusive approach, using resistivity technology to map subterranean remains over large areas — not unlike the scans of unborn children. But even when the diggers do get down to work, trenching and sieving and sorting and classifying, the results are often not much for viewers to look at. Remnants of dry stone walling, the corner of a building, some grubby sherds of pottery, at best a bit of rusty metal, or a coin worn smooth at the hands of history. The only way to bring these elements to life in a documentary film is to have someone tell stories about them; the better the stories, the better the programme. The story-tellers need to be knowledgeable, they need to be imaginative, and above all they need to be enthusiastic. It was Mick's passion for the past that had first drawn us to the idea of proposing a series of programmes about some of the places he knows best. In the Time Team format a group of experts 'parachute' in to a site, dig it in two or three days, and depart. The appeal of the programme lies in the artificial deadline it imposes on itself — a kind of commando raid on antiquity. The essential visual dullness of the sites is made exciting by rapid movements, fast cutting, and an atmosphere of mounting tension generated and sustained by presenter Tony Robinson and the rest of the team. In addition, massive resources of technology, computer graphics, and visiting experts help the viewer to 'see' what is being discovered. It is all a bit manic, but it is good story telling, and it pulls good audience figures.

With our modest regional television budget we couldn't muster a single computer image, but at the Kings of Wessex School, I surmised there would be a ready audience of students to listen to the story of the palace excavations. We might also try out some simple dramatisation of scenes from Saxon life. Who, I asked, at the school, should I talk to about that? History, they said. Head of History. Adrian Targett.

> *December 96* Contacted by Philip Priestley, of Epik television who is making a series of history and archaeology programmes on the local area for HTV. One of the programmes is to be about Cheddar and he wants to film in school for the bit in the programme about the Saxon Palace. Have got approval from the Head to do this. Philip Rahtz, the archaeologist who excavated the site in the 1960s, is going to 'explain' the site to the cameras: Philip P. thinks it will be a good idea to have some of our students in this sequence so that Rahtz has an audience.
> *Adrian Targett*

Now that was fixed, I turned to the other elements of the programme. There was an item about a mediaeval — it could even turn out to be Saxon — farmstead being dug by Mark Horton and his Bristol University students at Carscliffe Farm. There were also suggested Roman remains and other features of early urban Cheddar that needed exposition and Mick suggested another friend. Vince Russett, born and bred in the area, is archaeologist for North Somerset District Council. He was living in a house on his parents' farm at the edge of the town near the site of what might have been a Saxon port. He knew a lot about the old manor houses of Cheddar, and he had recently been looking at the industrial buildings along the stream that ran from under the cliffs at the bottom of the Gorge — water-driven textile mills, tanneries, and the like. There was a good interview to be had with him.

And then there were the caves. I went to Goughs or Cheddar Showcaves to give it and Cox's Cave their collective commercial title — and met the curator of its cave museum, Bob Smart. Bob was once pier-master at Clevedon. He has a fine line in dry wit, and cultivates the manner of a fully paid up English eccentric — another natural for a television programme. Early man, he thought, had come to Cheddar for some of the same reasons as modern visitors — 'limestone tourists' he called them. He was keen for the caves to feature in the film and we talked over what might go into it. The actual skeleton of Cheddar Man, he said, resided at the Natural History Museum in London under the care of Dr Chris Stringer, head of the Human Origins Group, and a pioneer of the view that modern human beings originated relatively recently in Africa and then spread rapidly across the globe. This is still a controversial thesis in palaeoanthropology, but it has a distinct bearing on the unfolding story of Cheddar Man. Chris Stringer had also undertaken a series of more recent excavations in Gough's Cave, unearthing burials of residents older than Cheddar Man. He was an obvious person to talk about the archaeology of the caves, but, and these are the realities of regional television budgets, he was in London and Cheddar is in the West Country. We were already committed to paying Philip Rahtz's fare from York and I didn't think we could afford to import another expert from afar. If you ever watch Horizon science programmes on BBC Television or environmental programmes on Discovery Channel you will notice shots that last a few seconds and which have obviously cost thousands of pounds to gather. If you watch HTV you will see whole half-hour documentaries that have cost less than those few seconds. Fine programmes too. This was going to be another of them.

Was there, I asked Mick Aston, anyone nearer at hand with an interest in this period? Larry Barham, he replied. Larry is very tall and comes from Texas. I thought he would be excellent in the film. He is knowledgeable, personable, and enthusiastic. He has discovered — in Africa — the most ancient use of pigments by human beings; the origins of art. More to the point he is Lecturer in Archaeology at the University of Bristol only 15 miles from Cheddar. I asked him if he would do a descriptive piece about the skeletons in the cave. He spoke to Chris Stringer on the phone and then agreed to be filmed talking to Mick in Gough's Cave about the kind of environment in which Cheddar Man, and the tribe or clan to which he belonged, had hunted and gathered and had children and died and been buried.

2 Becoming human

Human evolution, slow and steady, or short and sharp?

Some palaeoanthropologists see human evolution as a *gradual* process of change which has been underway from the very earliest ape-like ancestors to the appearance of Cheddar Man and his modern kin. Evolution has been slow, based on the accumulation of small changes in anatomy and behaviour over time. Others see a pattern of interrupted or *punctuated* change with new species evolving rapidly at moments of stress and replacing other, older species. Both views are compatible with the human evolutionary record. Our distant ancestor *Homo erectus*, who is the subject of this chapter, underwent a long and gradual development. Our own evolution, that of *Homo sapiens*, seems almost sudden by comparison — tens of thousands years is sudden in the long view — followed by our rapid spread across the Old World. This is the picture that the Out of Africa theory paints.

The rapid rise of new species — and the extinction of others — may result from dramatic changes in climate. Certainly the coming and going of ice ages profoundly altered the landscape of the Mendips and would have forced some hard choices on the Neanderthals and Cheddar Man's ancestors. But climate change has another important role in human origins. The ice ages created physical barriers, like deserts or glaciers, which separated populations of plants, animals and humans.

Geographical isolation can lead to the evolution of new species by interrupting the flow of genes between related groups of individuals. In other words, they no longer have the opportunity to mate. Over time two separated groups may change imperceptibly but significantly to the extent that when the barrier disappears the reunion goes badly; they are now incompatible in all sorts of ways. They may look different, smell different and behave in socially unacceptable ways in the eyes of the other (**9**). They are also probably genetically incompatible. Even if they wanted to mate, the outcome would be fruitless. This may have been the case when Cheddar Man's ancestors met Neanderthals for the first time.

But we are getting ahead of our story.

Adrian Targett has a long ancestry, the longest link so far made between a living human and a prehistoric individual. His link with Cheddar Man takes us back just over nine thousand years to near the end of the most recent ice age. That still leaves more than four million years of human evolution as the background to the Out of Africa debate, the fate of Neanderthals, and the link between Cheddar Man and us.

9   *Two long separated species, Neanderthals and modern humans, meet for the first time.*

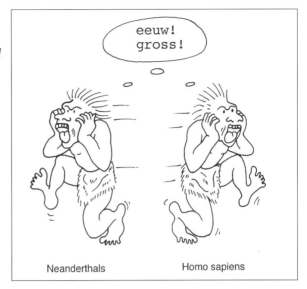

Two legs good, four legs bad

Our earliest ancestors evolved in Africa. A simple statement but an important one for the story which follows. We are essentially tropical animals which evolved in a tropical environment. The spread of humans into temperate latitudes and particularly into glacial Europe is all the more remarkable because of our origins. That northerly spread reveals much about what makes us such a successful species. Using stone tools, fire and language, our ancestors eventually colonised the Old and New worlds, with the exception of Antarctica. But the story of our success begins long before the first stone tools were made. What really makes us human and separates us from our ape ancestors is so basic that we take it for granted — walking.

Walking on two legs or *bipedalism* is something we do naturally and efficiently, except when arthritic or our mobility is otherwise impaired. Humans can run long distances, maybe not quickly compared with a sprinting cheetah, but without much effort. Chimpanzees, by comparison, waddle from side to side when walking upright and become tired quickly. For them, and all other apes, life is spent mostly on four legs. For climbing and moving about the forests of central Africa that is fine, their bodies are built for just such acrobatics. Our earliest ancestors evolved a bipedal way of living and we can recognise in their fossil skeletons the great changes in anatomy which took place as a consequence. One result of walking upright was that our hands were freed for carrying, for throwing, for making tools, for making gestures or just waving them about. Chimps do all these things but not as well as we do. Just when and why bipedalism evolved is important to know because it is a hallmark of our species.

Five million years ago Africa was covered in tropical woodland. The Sahara desert, which today is a formidable barrier separating north and central Africa, did not exist. In southern Africa, today's Kalahari region which is nearly a

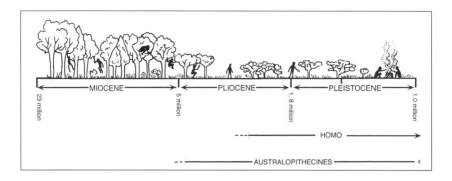

MIOCENE · PLIOCENE · PLEISTOCENE

23 million · 5 million · 1.8 million · 1.0 million

HOMO

AUSTRALOPITHECINES ———————— x

10   *The first bipedal apes (australopithecines) evolved 5 million years ago in the forests of Africa. The first stone tool-using ancestors (*Homo*) emerge about 2.5 million years ago in a more open and drier environment.* Homo erectus *may have been the first species to use fire and to spread out of Africa almost 2 million years ago. The australopithecines became extinct only 1 million years ago.*

desert, was a mix of open forest and grassland known as savannah. Most of Europe and Asia was forested. The world of 5 million years ago, known geologically as part of the late **Miocene** period (**10**), had not yet come under the clockwork spell of the ice ages, but a trend towards a generally cooler globe was underway. The late Miocene forests of the Old World were home to many species of ape. Some were the ancestors of today's gorillas and chimpanzees in Africa and the orang-utan and gibbons of south-east Asia.

We know that biologically the apes, in particular the chimpanzee, are our closest relations in the animal world. Genetically we are almost identical, with 98.9% of our DNA in common. Studying how chimpanzees live and behave today might enable us to understand the sorts of conditions in which walking on two legs became an advantage. Chimpanzees today are bipedal when trying to reach for fruits on branch tips of bushes and trees. They also stand up when throwing sticks and stones at each other or at predators such as leopards. The roots of bipedalism may lie in these two behaviours combined with the gradual break-up of the forests as the earth continued to become cooler and drier. In truth, despite the many current theories — there are at least eight — we do not really know how walking on two legs came about. The question of when it happened is easier to answer.

The differences which do exist between our DNA and that of chimps are estimated to have taken between 4-6 million years to accumulate, which suggests our last common ancestor probably lived about 5 million years ago. The fossil record from East Africa tells us much the same thing. The oldest fossil of a bipedal ancestor, so far, is 4.4 million years old but future research is likely to push this date back close to the 5 million mark. The earliest bipeds will be difficult to tell apart from apes because they will be so similar.

A younger and better known group of early bipeds called the Australopithecines ('southern ape men') was successful in adapting to new environments created by a changing climate. Between 4-2 million years ago the Australopithecines evolved into various species which spread into central

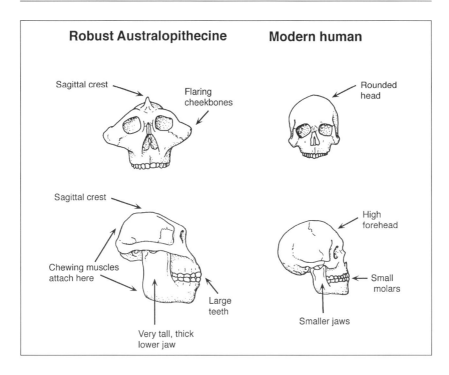

11   *A comparison of the robust skull and jaws of a plant-eating australopithecine with our own diminutive version (not to scale).*

and southern Africa. Some lived as vegetarians eating tough foods like nuts and shoots as well as leaves. Massive grinding teeth and large jaws — very effective nut crackers — were their trade mark, much like those of modern gorillas (**11**). Others ate a more mixed diet including leaves and fruit and perhaps a small amount of animal protein in the form of insects, lizards and the occasional small mammal. Their bodies were small and lightly built compared to their vegetarian cousins.

The late Miocene woodland home of the African apes and of our earliest ancestors had already begun to break apart and retreat. Between 2 and 3 million years ago, during the **Pliocene** period, the African climate changed: the dry seasons became longer, a mosaic landscape emerged composed of thick and thin forests and patches of open grassland. In this more open landscape our bipedal ancestors had a ready made advantage, they could walk between patches of woodland across grassland in search of food, water and shade during the heat of the day when most predators, such as lion, are snoozing.

Palaeoanthropologists Dean Falk and Peter Wheeler see bipedalism as a way of keeping the body cool and in particular preventing the brain from overheating. When standing upright we are exposed to less sun than an animal on all fours and have the benefit of having our brains as far from the heat of the ground as possible. The hair on our heads remains to protect us from sunstroke but we have shed our thick coat of body hair, unlike chimps. Our brains are also well 'ventilated' by a rich supply of blood which takes away heat like a water cooled car engine. Keeping cool also means needing less water and in a dry environment that is important. Overheating is a real danger in the tropics especially in open environments. Sunstroke can kill.

The same change in climate, which spurred the break-up of forests and the evolution of specialised nut cracking Australopithecines, may have also created an opening or *niche* for a tool-using biped who could scavenge the many animal carcasses to be found in the environment. The first stone tools appear 2.5 million years ago, just before the earliest evidence we have for our genus *Homo*. What earns early *Homo* the lofty status as our ancestor is its brain. The Australopithecines had brains the size of chimps, but early *Homo*'s is slightly larger even considering differences in body size. Could there be a link between tool use, meat eating and the evolution of larger-brained ancestors?

The first stone tools

Our ancestors were too slow and awkward to run down prey and lacked the claws and teeth to make an easy kill. Chimpanzees today hunt small monkeys using their skills as social animals to plan an ambush and brute force to tear apart the hapless victim. What chimps are not equipped to do is break open thick bones and extract the nutritious cholesterol-rich marrow. Fat is necessary for the proper working of the brain, but this essential food is scarce on the savannah grasslands where most animals are lean and oily nuts are available only seasonally. Bone marrow and brains provide a ready package of satisfying fats and they are available year round. But these packages come well wrapped. Breaking open bone requires a bit of thought. Hitting a bone against a rock is one method. Another, involving a bit more planning, uses a stone as an anvil and another as a hammer. The result is a splintered bone and sometimes a sharp flake of stone is accidentally struck off as the hammer hits the anvil. Stone flakes are excellent tools for cutting tough hides and for slicing meat from bones (**12**). Our distant ancestors may have learned this with the occasional cut finger — a painful but valuable lesson.

Having access to meat and marrow would be the key to the success of our genus *Homo*, as we will see, but stone tools also represent another human milestone — our dependency on *tools to make tools*. A simple flake can be used to shape other tools of wood, bone, antler and bark. For example, a stick whittled to a point makes a good tool for digging up edible bulbs, or a spear for hunting and protection. The beginning of our dependency on tools has its roots 2.5 million years ago in Africa.

Tool making also involves planning and learning. To start with, the right kind of stone for flaking or **knapping** has to be found. Experienced flint knappers today know that the best stone for making tools contains a high silica content, the same material used in making glass and computer chips. Silica-rich rocks, such as flint and quartz, break in predictable ways and produce consistently sharp and durable edges. With practice, the knapper

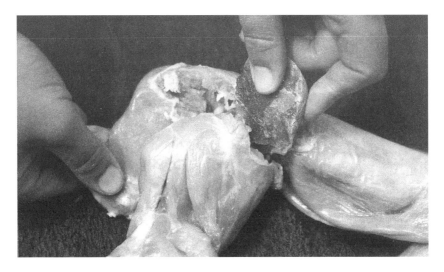

12   Butchering a rabbit (Bunny fluffy?) is easy with a sharp stone flake.

learns to co-ordinate the angle between the swing of the hammerstone and the surface of the stone to be struck or *core*. The length and thickness of the resulting flakes depends on the angle and force of the blow (**13**). Our early *Homo* ancestors had clearly grasped the geometry involved, something chimps and other apes find difficult to master.

A new boy in town

Tool making was at the root of another very human trait — our enormous brains. About 2 million years ago near the start of the **Pleistocene** period and the beginning of the ice ages, a new species of *Homo* evolved.

Homo erectus had a larger body and brain than earlier forms of *Homo*. We know a surprising amount about early *Homo erectus* thanks to the remarkable discovery of a nearly complete skeleton found near Lake Turkana in northern Kenya. Kenyan conservationist and palaeoanthropologist Richard Leakey and his colleague Alan Thorne pieced together the many fragments to reveal a surprisingly human-like body of a boy who lived 1.5 million years ago.

The 'Turkana Boy' was tall for an eleven-year-old at 5ft 3in (1.6m) and had he lived to be an adult he would have been 6ft 1in tall (1.8m). His long legged body was well suited to the heat of the tropical savannah, acting as a natural radiator. The brain and body were twice as large as his early *Homo* ancestors, but the Turkana boy was still not fully modern. The skull and therefore the brain of *Homo erectus* was two-thirds the size of ours and was shaped differently, being long and squat to our round and high skull. For most modern humans, the left hemisphere of the brain contains specialised areas which enable us to speak and to comprehend speech. These areas are larger in the left hemisphere than in the right with the result that our brains are slightly asymmetrical (**14**). The left hemisphere also controls the right-hand

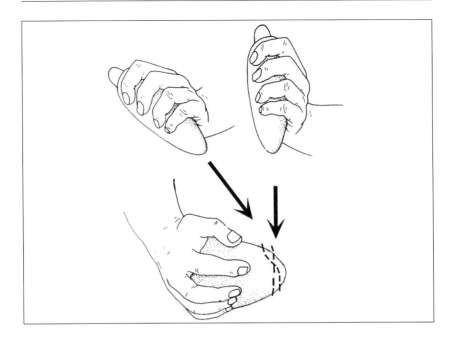

13   *Making flakes and complex tools like handaxes involves an understanding of the angle of the hammer blow, the force of the blow and the shape of the core.*

side of our bodies so that right-handed people are left-brained, and, conversely, left-handed people are in their right minds. The terrible pun aside, a close evolutionary link seems to exists between language, tool-use, right-handedness and brain asymmetry. Casts of the interior of *erectus* skulls, and of the Turkana specimen itself, demonstrate that left hemisphere asymmetry had emerged with this species.

The *erectus* skull also had a thick bony shelf over the eyes. With his massive brow ridges the Turkana Boy would certainly stand out in a crowd today and if you spoke to him, assuming he understood English, the conversation might be a bit one-sided. The left hemisphere assymetry of his skull leads us to expect an ancestor with developed language skills. His spine tells a different story — *Homo erectus* had a limited ability to speak.

Our vertebrae are shaped like ring doughnuts with a hollow to carry the spinal cord to and from the brain. In the Turkana boy the opening of the vertebrae is narrower than ours and from this evidence it seems unlikely that the boy had the fine control over his breathing needed to produce words and speak clearly by our standards. That is not to say he could not speak. *Homo erectus* communication was probably about the here and now, expressing wants and emotions and giving names to things, places and people. Complex thoughts about future plans, past events or concepts such as right and wrong might have been beyond the grasp of *erectus* language. Perhaps they were not needed.

The large size of the Turkana boy for his age suggests his growth pattern was more like that of apes than modern humans. Ape children grow at a

14 *A simplified cross-section of the modern human brain showing the asymmetry between the left and right hemispheres and the location of some important language areas (grey).*

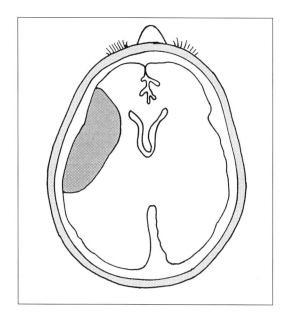

regular rate and do not experience an adolescent growth spurt like ours. Some palaeoanthropologists have speculated that our delayed growth pattern is useful in giving children extra time as children. It means they are not seen as competitors by adults for food, mates and status and it also gives children added time for learning what is involved in being a full fledged member of a particular community. If you live in a socially and technologically complex world then an extra few years for learning would be to your and everyone's advantage. *Homo erectus* was not yet living in such a world.

Toolkit for the traveller

What *Homo erectus* lacked in eloquence, this ancestor made up for by its intelligence and use of tools. *Erectus* had a far larger bag of tricks for harnessing energy from the environment than any of its competitors. The brightest tool in this bag was fire. The earliest evidence for the use of fire comes from Africa at the time of the Turkana boy — about 1.5 million years ago. At the cave of Swartkrans in South Africa, the excavator Bob Brain found hundreds of blackened and charred animal bones along with stone tools made by *erectus*. By experimenting with modern bones in ovens, Brain showed that the Swartkrans bones had been burnt at high temperatures like those of a camp fire. The burning was not accidental. Other sites showing an early use of fire have been found in east Africa, Swartkrans is not alone. Fire has some obvious benefits like providing heat for cooking, keeping warm and frightening away dangerous beasts. Cooking is especially important not just because it makes meat easier to chew but because it kills bacteria, which extends the shelf life of a side of elephant considerably. Some savannah plants also contain natural poisons which cooking destroys.

Fire offers a less obvious but socially important benefit — light. The daily routine for most daytime-active animals is to wake up with the sun and go to sleep with the dark. A campfire breaks nature's routine. *Homo erectus* was the first ancestor able to stay up past bedtime. Fire extends the working day but also provides a focus for the group, a place to gather for gossip and to exchange information about the environment. The fireside is also a good place to tell stories that entertain and teach a lesson. Perhaps Swartkrans was just such a camp.

Story telling is important in societies without writing. It is a way of teaching the young the history and traditions of a group. Through traditions the young learn — and others are reminded — what is expected of them and how to behave properly according to that group's standards. In a small community it is essential for the group's survival that everyone knows what is considered acceptable behaviour. This is the essence of human society. It is a set of shared standards of right and wrong, good and bad, duties and obligations which make social life predictable and productive. Language plays an important role in the development of shared concepts like good and bad, and ultimately in the emergence of human culture.

We can never know if the Turkana boy heard stories around the campfire, or took part in what would be a recognisably human form of culture. Perhaps the real significance of fire for human social evolution is that it created a new context for learning and for enhancing a sense of belonging to a group. Maybe this was the context in which language and culture emerged.

If nothing else, we know *Homo erectus* was an accomplished tool maker. The simple flakes and choppers of earlier times were still being made but a new and more complicated tool appears with *erectus*. Called a handaxe, this tool is pear-shaped with a pointed tip and a rounded base and because it does fit the hand nicely it may have been used just as it was, that is without a handle (**15**). Handaxes are not easy to make. To get the pear shape involves removing flakes from both sides of the piece with each flake scar used as the striking surface for the next flake. To get a fairly straight edge and to make a symmetrical pear shape involves planning. The consequences of each flake removal have to be *anticipated* because mistakes are difficult to fix in stone. Learning by watching others and by trial and error are probably the way most knappers acquired the skill to make handaxes. Direct teaching by talking the beginner through the steps of knapping might also have been important, but as we have seen with the Turkana boy, language for early *erectus* was probably short on concepts.

Regardless of how the skill was acquired, making handaxes was something *Homo erectus* did well and for a long time. These tools were made for more than 1 million years (from 1.4 million to 300,000 years ago in Africa) without great changes to the basic design. Modern experiments show why the handaxe kept its shape: it was a brilliant tool for butchering. The heavy cutting edges could slice through thick hides and tough tendons, just the thing for making mince meat of an elephant. A handaxe can also be used for that very human trait: making tools to make other tools.

The handaxe is a signature of *Homo erectus* and where we find these artefacts we can be reasonably sure that this ancestor made them, at least the early ones

15   A typical flint handaxe from Swanscombe, Kent.

before 500,000 years ago. After this date, *erectus* has descendants in Africa and Europe who by 200,000 years ago are no longer relying on handaxes (see Chapter 4).

Handaxes are found not just in Africa but in Europe, the Middle East and India but rarely further east into Asia. *Homo erectus* was a globetrotter and the first human species to leave Africa. (This is not the same event as in the Out of Africa theory which concerns our direct ancestor *Homo sapiens*, that took place much later.) Early in its evolution, about 1.8 million years ago, *erectus* spread from Africa into Asia following a tropical route. The environment of the Middle East and parts of India was similar to that of east Africa with a mix of grassland and tropical woodland with similar animals including ostrich and antelopes. Groups of *Homo erectus* spread gradually eastwards following familiar animals and plants and by 1.6 million years had reached Java in south-east Asia, more than 8,000 miles (12,800km) from the African homeland. These Asian *erectus* groups did not make handaxes. Perhaps they left Africa before handaxes became standard issue or they used local Asian materials such as bamboo for making tools. Bamboo with its tough hard covering can cut and scrape like a stone tool and it grows in a variety of environments but, like most plants, it is unlikely to survive in the archaeological record.

A recipe for success

Homo erectus lasted more than a million years and colonised most of the Old World. Why was this species so successful? The answer lies partly in biology and partly in behaviour. The Turkana boy showed us that *erectus* individuals were large and efficient bipeds. They could walk or run long distances and keep cool. This trait was important in finding new patches of food and especially in hunting animals. This latter aspect of our development is crucial. At some critical point in our evolution we became meat eaters. As vegetarians, or simply scavengers as opposed to hunters, it is arguable we would never have survived in the cold and inhospitable northern hemisphere.

Just when this carnivorous change happened is still hotly argued. Some palaeoanthropologists think there is very little evidence for organised hunting until long after *Homo erectus* became extinct. For them, the first real hunters were ourselves, anatomically modern humans. Most meat in the diet of *Homo erectus*, according to this argument, came from scavenging. Others argue that hunting has long been part of the human adaptation, and that by the time of *erectus* meat was an established part of the diet.

Leslie Aiello, a palaeoanthropologist at University College, London, explains that the brain demands a large amount of energy from the body and our brains are especially large for the size of our bodies. The modern human brain is three times larger than it need be given our body size. It clearly was an important organ in our evolution. But the brain is expensive to run because it uses so much energy. Aiello argues that until our ancestors added meat and marrow to their diets the human brain was constrained from becoming much larger than that of the Australopithecines or chimps today. Meat and marrow provide an easily digestible source of energy and nutrients. We can choose to be vegetarians today because of the wide range of fruits, vegetables, pulses and grains available to us through supermarkets, not to mention expensive vitamin supplements. That option is less easy to choose on the grasslands of east Africa or India and even more difficult in the harsh climate of glacial Europe. The robustly built Australopithecines with their large teeth and jaws could cope with tough plant foods. The modern gorilla which is a vegetarian also has the teeth and jaw muscles to crunch woody stalks and stems and an unusual stomach with an extra chamber to digest plant fibres, much like a cow. *Homo erectus* had neither of these specialisations, but did have tools and intelligence.

Both could have been put to good use in making a living as a professional scavenger on the African savannah. The big cats like lion and leopard when they make a kill, feast on the meatiest parts and leave the marrow-rich bones, skin and tendons behind. A clever scavenger could just about make a living from these table scraps with a bit of planning. Rob Blumenschine, a palaeoanthropologist at Rutgers University in New Jersey, has looked at today's east African savannah to find out just where and when animal carcasses would have been available to a scavenger. His research shows that during the long dry season when food and water is scarce, animals gather around waterholes, streams and lakes. Here the big cats make their kills. These scraps could make all the difference between starvation and survival to a small biped like early *Homo*, but large bodied *Homo erectus* needed something more than leftovers. Leslie Aiello and others argued that they were hunters and that eating meat fed their brains and their bodies.

Meat provides a rich source of protein and energy which is conveniently packaged and stored in the form of animals. Large numbers of big mammals,

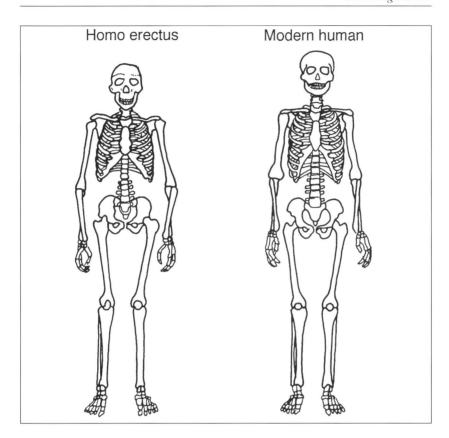

Homo erectus   Modern human

16   *The ribcage of the Turkana boy (left) is similar in shape to ours (right), suggesting that meat was an established part of the human diet by 1.5 million years ago.*

antelopes in particular, are a feature of the grasslands of Africa and India. The savannah provides a walking supermarket boasting a wide selection of tasty creatures. For the biped who could hunt this was Eden. Hunting by modern humans involves a web of related activities including making and using weapons, stalking or ambushing game which means understanding their behaviour, working as a group during the hunt and cooperating afterwards in dividing up the meat and marrow. Scavenging also involves planning and is more effective with some help from others but hunting is even more demanding, both physically and mentally. A brain which could integrate the planning and the doing would make hunting a successful strategy. The reward would be protein, energy and a full stomach during the long dry season. At some point a trade off was made between organs competing for energy in the body and the brain. The brain won at the expense of the gut. Our intestines and stomach are about half the capacity they should be for our body size.

In the upper body of the Turkana boy we see an echo of the shift to meat eating. Apes today have, and the Australopithecines had, flaring chests

33

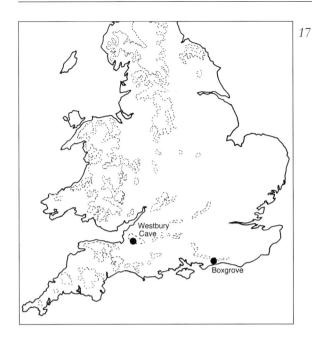

17   *The 500,000-year-old sites of Boxgrove (West Sussex) and Westbury Cave (Somerset) are the earliest in Britain and some of the oldest in Europe.*

designed to protect the heart and lungs but also their big guts. The ape ribcage is at its widest here. Our rib cage is more tapered around the stomach and intestines which reflects the smaller size of these organs. The Turkana boy had the human shape of ribcage (**16**) which tells us that by 1.5 million years ago meat was probably a regular part of the diet.

Horse meat for dinner

Back in Britain, what evidence do we have for the importance of meat in the diet of Cheddar Man's distant *erectus* ancestors? Leaping forward a million years to around 500,000 years ago, the remarkable archaeological site of Boxgrove in West Sussex (**17**) gives us a clue. Boxgrove is today a sand and gravel quarry, but half a million years ago it was a grassy open plain sandwiched between the sea and high chalk cliffs. Pools of fresh water attracted animals including herds of horse and rhinoceros. Near these pools, preserved in fine sediments are their bones and the tools used to butcher them. The bones show signs of butchering in the form of *cut marks* left by the sharp edge of flint handaxes. A flint cutting edge leaves a clear furrow in fresh bone which looks different from the marks left by the teeth of scavengers. The location of cut marks on the skeleton can be an important clue to whether the animal was hunted or scavenged. Scavengers tend to get the leftovers, the meaty parts are eaten first by hunters, whether lion or human. At Boxgrove, the cut marks are overlain by gnaw marks; the humans got to the animal first. The well-preserved skeleton of one particular horse reveals a full sequence of related events from the initial kill, the disjointing of the limbs, the removal of prized parts such as the tongue and the final smashing of the bone to extract marrow. These were not simple scavengers.

18   A freshly excavated handaxe from Boxgrove, West Sussex.

Several piles of flint flakes were found around the horse's body. When the flakes were fitted together it became clear that they had come from handaxes (**18**), but the handaxes were nowhere to be found. It seems that after the horse was stripped clean the Boxgrove people took their finished tools with them, perhaps back to a camp somewhere on the downs overlooking the plains. The living areas of these people have not been found but Boxgrove has provided unrivalled insights into the capabilities of people living far north of their ancestral African home 500,000 years ago. Mark Roberts, the project director, makes a convincing argument based on the archaeological finds and from practical experiments that these people were hunting large and dangerous game — rhinos are frightening today even from the security of a Land Rover — with the help of wooden spears.

Wood rarely survives from these very early periods but in 1997 it was announced that seven beautifully preserved spears made of spruce had been discovered at the German site of Schöningen, in what is now a quarry. The Schöningen spears are carefully made being more than 6ft (2m) long and deftly balanced like a modern javelin (**19**). They are 400,000 years old, the earliest wooden tools anywhere. The tips are shaved to points. The fact that they were found with thousands of horse bones, many with butchering marks, suggests spears like this might have been used to kill the Boxgrove horse. A neat hole in its shoulder blade was made by an object thrown with force. This kind of evidence and that of the spears themselves shows these ancestors to have been capable of hunting large game.

The tip of yew spear was found early in the twentieth century at Clacton-on-Sea, Essex, in deposits laid down by an old channel of the river Thames. The Clacton spear is not as old as the Schöningen finds, the associated animal bones are from an interglacial period about 250,000 years ago, but it reminds

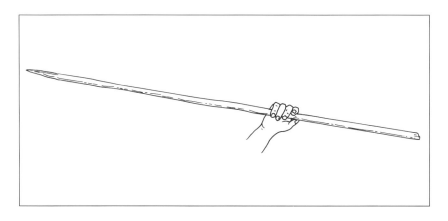

19   *A javelin-like wooden spear from Schöningen, Germany. The spear is carefully shaped with the weight concentrated in the front third.*

us that only a small range of objects made by our ancestors actually survive. Most sites, especially those in the open, are poor environments for the preservation of organic artefacts of wood, bone, antler, bark and hide. The roles these materials played in the lives of early humans can only be the subject of educated guesswork. Only much later with anatomically modern human is it certain that bone and antler were important raw materials.

The study of how archaeological sites form and how they change is called **taphonomy**. Understanding how a site formed and has been altered is an essential piece of detective work that every archaeologist must consider before making interpretations about the past. Very rarely are archaeological sites preserved just as they were left by humans. The horse butchery area at Boxgrove is one and Pompeii is another. These are the exceptions to the rule. Humans, just by living on sites, cause an immense amount of disturbance to the evidence they leave behind. Making fires, digging rubbish pits, clearing a sleeping area, levelling a floor — these are just a few of things humans do which churn and mix deposits. Animals too are destructive by their trampling of surfaces, digging of burrows and nest making. Termites constructing their huge mounds can be extremely disruptive, but even the humble earthworm can cause artefacts to move from their original resting places by its turning of the soil.

Caves are especially vulnerable to disturbance. Not only do they attract people and animals in search of shelter, caves as fixed points on the landscape are heavily used for long periods of time. Their floors are often a mixture of sediments and artefacts from different periods of time. A rushed excavation can create very misleading results.

The often complex pattern of human and animal use of caves makes the study of cave taphonomy a demanding but vital task if our interpretations of the past are to be meaningful. A classic case, and one relevant to the issue of the human settlement of northern Europe, comes from the site of Westbury quarry, over the top of the Mendips and to the south of Gough's Cave.

Bones and stones in Westbury Cave

Humans were at Boxgrove, there is no doubt about it: we have their artefacts and their teeth and bones. In the case of Westbury Cave, there is considerable doubt. The large cave is the same age as Boxgrove, but there are no handaxes or human bones just a fine collection of animal bones and 357 pieces of flint which may or may not be artefacts. Understanding how the bones and stones came to be found together is essential to detecting whether humans used the cave.

Westbury Cave lay hidden from view until exposed by blasting in 1969 when the quarry was extended. The bones of an extinct cave-dwelling bear and cave lion and other large animals tumbled down the quarry face along with flint flakes. This was clearly an early and important fossil site. If the flints were artefacts then Westbury could lay claim to being the oldest site in Britain, if not in Europe. The recent discoveries at Boxgrove have taken the spotlight away from Westbury, but the site is still important as potential evidence for understanding how early humans used the landscape.

As blasting continued a large rescue excavation was mounted by the Natural History Museum, London, between 1976-84 to record what survived of the cave and its contents. This was no ordinary excavation. The team of experts worked on the vertical quarry face, secured by ropes like mountain climbers, suspended 100ft (30m) above the quarry floor (**20**). The results were surprising: Westbury Cave was rich in animal bone but poor in flint tools. Maybe this was a 'bone cave' like so many others found in the region and not a place where humans lived for any length of time, if at all.

The main chamber of Westbury Cave is huge, measuring 200ft (60m) long, 80ft (25m) wide and 100ft (30m) deep. It resembles caves still forming today in the Mendips from the combined erosional effects of rainwater and underground streams. Rain is naturally slightly acidic and when it falls onto Mendip limestone it gradually eats away at the calcium-rich rock. The dissolving effect of rainwater is especially active along the many cracks or faults in the heavily folded limestones of the region. Over time the cracks widen through chemical and physical erosion, becoming fissures which can become caves. Depending on the level of the water table, underground streams can be major players in the creation of cave systems. Five hundred thousand years ago, Westbury Cave opened to the outside environment and began to fill with sediments washed in from the surrounding landscape. The cave also became the home of wild animals such as cave bear and lion. Barn owls, long-eared owls and eagle owls made the cave their home as well. Together, the large and small mammals enable us to piece together the changing landscape and climate of 500,000 years ago.

Owls are important in this story. They eat small mammals, usually mice and voles. We know that these small mammals today prefer certain kinds of plant cover for food and protection. The plant cover itself reflects the local environment and also the climate of the region. If we can recognise which species lived at the site in the past we can use living relatives to reconstruct the ancient environment. Peter Andrews of the Natural History Museum has

37

20   *Westbury Cave, Somerset, is today a treacherous cliff face on the edge of a
quarry. The thick and complex sequence of deposits contains well preserved
bones of extinct forms of bear, lion and voles and perhaps stone tools.*

done just this for Westbury Cave. His reconstruction shows that the local area
was home to a variety of rodents including voles, mice and lemmings. The
changing species of voles in particular reflect a complex sequence of
environmental shifts on the Mendips during one or more interglacial periods.
Certain voles favour open grassland and others more wooded habitats. The
sequence of vole bones at Westbury shows a warm interglacial like today with
two cold snaps or stadials, with a final shift toward glacial conditions and a
tundra environment which was home to lemmings. (This record of climate
change matches that seen in the Greenland ice cores for the most recent
interglacial which lasted from 127,000 to 117,000 years ago.) The voles are
also vital for dating Westbury Cave. The age estimate of 500,000 years is based
on the presence of a genus of vole called *Arvicola*. This group of voles has a
distinctive feature — their molar teeth have no roots. The lack of roots may
seem trivial but in the world of small mammal palaeontology it is hugely
important. The ancestors of *Arvicola* had molars with roots and they lived just
before 500,000 years ago. *Arvicola* appears just after or thereabouts. The
change from roots to no roots is an evolutionary event and one which marks
a point in time.

The Westbury Cave animals — large and small — tell us that humans living
at Boxgrove 500,000 years ago did so during an interglacial much like any
other during the past 700,000 years. The bears and voles of Westbury provide
a fascinating and wonderfully detailed record of a landscape distant in time,
but where were the humans in this interglacial world? Boxgrove has

abundant evidence for humans hunting and butchering animals on the Sussex downs, but why not Westbury Cave? There is controversy over the evidence which, like Boxgrove, comes in the form of flint artefacts and cut marks on bone. Today the Mendip hills are a poor source of flint. This basic material of stone age life does not occur naturally in pieces large enough or of suitable quality for making tools. Assuming that the same conditions existed 500,000 years ago then how did pieces of flint find their way into the cave? The flints are mostly small flakes, like those made when knapping flint to make larger tools. These would be the leftovers or waste flakes. But the evidence is not so straightforward. Flakes can sometimes be struck naturally by the force of running water or by a fast moving mud flow which bangs cobbles together. Most if not all of the 'artefacts' from Westbury may have been created by such natural forces.

Jill Cook of the British Museum, who has studied the Westbury flints closely, sees little convincing evidence that humans were involved. She notes that most of the flakes are small and the 'cores' have scars which could have been made naturally. Many archaeologists disagree and argue that some of the cores have just too many flake scars to be accidental (**21**), and that some flakes look like handaxe trimmings. Humans seem to have been responsible for at least some of the flint artefacts. They also point out that flint is not found naturally on the Mendips and has to be brought in, perhaps from Wiltshire or Devon. Cook argues that small pockets of flint do occur on Mendip and that one of these may have simply washed into Westbury Cave. If a single handaxe had been found like those from Boxgrove then there would be no debate, Westbury Cave would be an archaeological site. But nothing so obviously human has been found and the site remains an enigma.

Before leaving Westbury, mention must be made of one bone — and perhaps as many as four — from the cave which has cut marks like those made by flint tools at Boxgrove. The bone belonged to the lower leg of a red deer. The leg had been butchered by a human using a flint tool. The shape of the cut marks, their placement on the bone and the direction of the slicing are conclusive — this was a deliberate, planned act and not an accident of nature. But why just one butchered bone from a collection of more than 5,000 animal bones? Perhaps people did not live in the cave, which was home to dangerous lions and bears, but used the cave mouth just occasionally as a temporary shelter. A small group of people camping for a week or so would leave very few tools and little in the way of food refuse. Some of their rubbish might gradually be washed into the cave and become mingled with the mess created by denning bears. One or two stays near the cave could account for all the flint artefacts and cut bone found. This vision of Westbury as a stone age motel is not especially convincing, it relies too much on unsupported guesswork. Further excavations concentrated around the two suspected entrances might resolve the lingering questions about early humans on Mendip.

Westbury quarry today is being gradually transformed into a site for visitors and may one day be open to the public. What survives has been designated a Site of Special Scientific Interest in recognition of its international

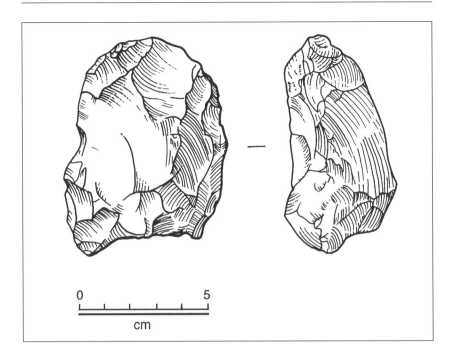

21 One of the most contentious 'artefacts' from Westbury Cave. Was it made by a human or by nature? (after Bishop 1975).

importance as a source of fossil bones and environmental information. It is also a classic example of archaeological detective work in the name of taphonomy.

Into the cold north winds

Just when and how humans arrived in Europe is currently a subject of heated debate. As Boxgrove shows, people were in northern Europe by half a million years ago. The debate is about how much earlier people arrived and how convincing is the evidence. Most archaeologists accept that if humans were in Europe much before 500,000 BP they were few in number because they left little in the way of artefacts and bones. After 500,000 BP there is plenty of evidence. A small but growing number of archaeologists support a 'long chronology' for *Homo erectus* in Europe, one going back more than a million years. The evidence for such an early arrival comes from southern Europe, mostly from sites in Spain and Italy (**22**).

Two Spanish sites, Orce in the south-east and Atapuerca in north-central Spain are the most controversial. At Orce, two separate clusters of about one hundred simple stone artefacts each — mostly flakes and choppers — have been found. One cluster was found near the bones of a hippopotamus: could this be a butchery site? The importance of these two groups of artefacts is that they come from sediments deposited about 1.8 million years ago. That makes

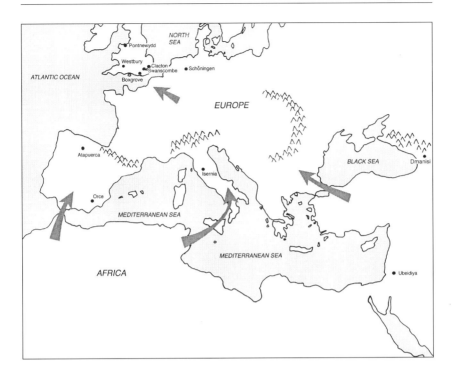

22   *Some of the earliest archaeological sites in Europe and possible routes of entry for humans from Africa and the Middle East.*

them by far the earliest tools found in Europe, if indeed they are genuine artefacts. Just like at Westbury, there is some doubt whether the Orce flakes and cores are humanly made or natural products. Human remains have also been reported from Orce but not all palaeoanthropologists are convinced that the skull bones are definitely human; they resemble those of a young horse. Sites of this age rightly deserve close scrutiny not just because they are rare but because, if accepted as genuine, they change our perceptions about the behaviour of *Homo erectus*.

Atapuerca's claim for early humans in Europe is currently the more convincing. The site itself is a set of caves in a limestone plateau in central Spain. At one cave, Gran Dolina in an archaeological layer labelled TD6, human remains have been found with simple stone tools beneath a layer dated to 780,000 BP. Assuming the order of the deposits has not been disturbed, the layers at the bottom of the site are older than the ones above. This makes the artefacts and human bones older — perhaps much older — than 780,000 years. The bones have been classified as a new species of *Homo*, but they come from a juvenile. It is hard to say whether an adult specimen would be so different from *erectus* as to be worthy of a new species title. The date of Gran Dolina remains controversial, but there is growing acceptance that the site provides evidence of an early human presence in southern Europe.

These southern European sites are the strongest contenders for establishing when *Homo erectus* first appeared in Europe. Future research may turn up more but for time being the evidence seems to show an early entry into southern Europe by 800,000 years ago and only later, by 500,000 years ago, did humans settle further north. Perhaps the delay was necessary to give a tropical species time to adjust to a temperate climate. Boxgrove shows that hunting big game was part of the solution.

Finally, the question of *how* humans entered Europe is important because the route chosen tells us something about the intelligence of *Homo erectus*. Two routes are possible: one by land, moving from Turkey across the Bosphorus, the other route by sea (**22**).

Having walked from Turkey and into south-eastern Europe, our ancestors faced a mountainous task, literally, in moving north. The main European mountain masses — the Carpathians, Alps and Pyrenees — run from east to west and are a formidable barrier to northward migrations. Mountain glaciers, not to mention extreme cold and lack of game would have made an ice age entry unlikely. More plausible would have been a trickle of humans moving slowly across southern Europe, following herds of game, during a warm phase when conditions were more to the liking of *erectus*. The discovery of a *Homo erectus* jaw in Georgia at the site of Dmanisi shows that humans were on the margins of Europe by perhaps 1.4 million years ago. The Dmanisi jaw also raises the possibility of another land route into Europe through the Caucasus mountains and across the plains of eastern Europe. That would be the colder option, but one rich in game.

The watery route includes island hopping across the Mediterranean from North Africa into Italy or a short 7-mile (12km) boat ride from Morocco to Gibraltar. Sea levels were lower during glacial periods and would have exposed more land in the Mediterranean but there would still be some sea to cross. An open water crossing would require some planning and probably a degree of communication or language which most archaeologists think *Homo erectus* did not possess, but perhaps we should not underestimate the abilities of this world travelling ancestor who was island hopping across Indonesia 700,000 years ago.

The successful settlement of Europe by *Homo erectus* was a landmark in human evolution. Tropical in origin, *Homo erectus* applied its large brain and physical skills to meeting the many new challenges of life in ice age Europe. The eating of meat, whether gained by scavenging or hunting, was crucial to the survival of this species especially as it moved ever northward. Fire and clothing of some sort would also be part of the success story. Language, or at least some form of practical communication would probably have been essential to the planning and co-ordination of successful hunts of dangerous animals such as rhinoceros.

There are no living parallels for modelling the intellect of *erectus*. We also have few clues about how they organised their social lives. Did they live like some hunter-gatherers today in co-operative bands of related families which share food and have a sense of community? Probably not is the working answer. The discovery of campsites with the quality of preservation of

Boxgrove would go some way toward answering this question.

What can be said of European *erectus* is that this species arrived and thrived. It built on a basic repertoire of tools and abilities developed for a tropical world and designed strategies for coping with rapid changes from open tundra to forest and the many stages in-between. Ice age Europe would provide the evolutionary stimulus which shaped descendants of *erectus* into the distinctly cold-adapted species we call Neanderthal.

DRILLING FOR HISTORY

As the television series took shape I remembered an earlier conversation with Tom Archer at HTV when I had speculated about drilling Cheddar Man for DNA and then testing some Cheddar residents to see if any of them were descended from him. I asked around and was given the name of Bryan Sykes at the Institute of Molecular Medicine — situated in the Radcliffe Hospital and part of Oxford University. Bryan's main work is in the genetics of cystic fibrosis, he told me on the phone, but he had developed a substantial side-line in ancient DNA. He worked closely with Chris Stringer at the Natural History Museum and had already had one go at getting DNA from the bones of Cheddar Man. They had drilled his big toe and come up with — super-glue! No sign of genetic material. He was more than willing to try again — this time on one of CM's molars — dentine being a much more likely repository of DNA. And testing Cheddar residents would be no problem either — in fact members of his team were already gathering samples for a large-scale genetic mapping project of the British Isles.

How much, I wondered, would all that cost. I held my breath. One thousand pounds for drilling the jaw and sequencing any DNA that might be there, he said. And one thousand pounds for despatching two colleagues to Cheddar to test 20 residents and sequence the results. Two thousand pounds altogether. I held my breath again. Pleaded poverty. Any chance of a cheaper deal? Two thousand pounds was a significant proportion of the budget total for the programme, in fact an appreciable item for the series as a whole. 'No,' he said, 'no chance of a reduction.' Retrieving and analysing ancient DNA was a lengthy and time-consuming process — took months to complete. But what he would agree to do was to drill the jaw and if no DNA was found he would make no charge. Obviously then there would be no testing in Cheddar either. I said I would think about it, talk to my colleague in EPIK TV, and come back to him.

Harvey was enthusiastic. 'Go for it,' he said. It was a risk. But even if we over-spent it would be a good story. Even if we didn't strike gold, failed to get a positive result — there would still be an interesting story to tell about the way in which the science of DNA can be used in modern archaeology.

Friday 22 November 1996. I am in Ireland. I send a fax to Bryan Sykes agreeing his terms and asking him to proceed with the work on Cheddar Man. I also send a copy to Chris Stringer at the Natural History Museum so that they can liaise over the transport of the jaw to Oxford.

Time passed. We shot scenes in the caves. Larry Barham, silhouetted against the cave wall, told Mick Aston about the burials, the rituals. Chris Stringer's excavations had revealed the bones of what appeared to be a family buried together. There were two adults and two children, all of them about four thousand years older than Cheddar Man. Many of the bones showed signs of butchery and 'de-fleshing'. Maybe there had been some sacramental eating of the dead. They discussed the ideological and cultural bases of so-called primitive societies, about their possible affluence, and about the coming of agriculture.

> *Friday 13 December* Have selected about half a dozen Year 9 pupils to be Professor Rahtz's 'students'. The television team arrive at about a quarter to two, comprising Philip P., Professor Rahtz, Professor Mick Aston (of Channel 4 Time Team fame) who is the 'front man' for the programme, camera woman and sound recordist. Introduce our year 9s to all of them. One of the Year 9s, Sam Astell, soon has everyone at their ease, informing Mick that Time Team is his favourite programme, and where is Tony Robinson — and a lot more questions. Afternoon spent taking a variety of shots of Rahtz and Aston talking and walking round the Palace site, then of the students with them asking questions and finally with the students standing on the post hole blocks, acting as human markers. Some of the film team believe our year 9s must be Rahtz's youngest ever students, 'He's not taught anything younger than undergraduates,' says one. In fact, in conversation with me, he says that he taught at Greenbank School in Bristol for some years, and in the film sequences the kids hang on his every word. By now — 4.00pm — the light is failing, so we go inside. Show the team some colour enlargements of the site taken whilst it was being excavated. Rahtz talks us through what they show and the camera woman 'shoots' them. Leave at 4.30. *Adrian Targett*

We also went up the tower of the parish church with Vince Russett. He gave Mick a tour d'horizon of the Gorge and the settlements below; Neolithic finds; a likely Roman settlement under the Victorian Vicarage below the tower; the shape of the Saxon townscape beyond the school.

'Your family, Vince,' Mick said to him finally, 'has been here for a very long time, hasn't it?' Vince spoke of his great grandmother on his mother's side, Daisy Starr. Starr is an ancient Cheddar surname, traceable back to the eleventh century. 'There's been Starrs in Cheddar, m'dear,' he remembers her saying, ' since we came out of the caves.' Mick and Vince both laugh. Behind the camera I did a little jig. What a story! Let Vince be descended from Cheddar Man, I pray. Let Vince be the one. I implore him to come and have his DNA tested, and his mum if she will. This is mitochondrial DNA we are after. It comes down the female line of descent. An archaeologist born and bred and still living in Cheddar, with a local name going back to Norman times, and a family joke that might have been quarried from folk-memory or the collective unconscious. It just had to be him!

One evening, after filming in the village, we went up to the Gorge which was closed to traffic and to the public for its annual spring-clean when loose limestone is scoured from the rock-faces. The light was fading fast. We hastily filmed Mick against the rocks doing a piece to camera to introduce the DNA sequence. 'Cheddar Man,' he says, 'has not yielded up all his secrets, even now.' Then Jill Ranford turned her camera down the Gorge to catch the dying of the day. Bob Smart, the Cave Museum curator told me he often watches as the sun sets between the cliffs, wondering if Cheddar Man did the same when he was here. Tonight the sky was gold and blue, and the evening air filled with bird-song, enchanting as choristers in a hushed cloister. Nick Turner pointed his microphone in that direction and we took several minutes of it.

3 The Neanderthal connection

The humans who left their tools at Boxgrove and possibly at Westbury Cave were not our direct ancestors. The evidence is a robust human shinbone, found at Boxgrove in 1993. A lot can be learned from a single bone. The Boxgrove individual, probably male, was in his twenties, 6ft (1.8m) tall, weighed 12½ stones (80kg) and was very strong. Such a tall heavy body is an *erectus* legacy which had its roots at the time of the Turkana boy, but the individual is not of the *erectus* species. The 500,000-year-old Boxgrove specimen comes at the beginning of a European lineage which soon develops distinctive physical traits which set it apart from African and Asian archaic humans. It is thought by Chris Stringer and other palaeoanthropologists to be an early fossil of *Homo heidelbergensis*.

The bone is similar to ones found at sites in France, Germany, Spain, Greece and Britain that were part of a widespread species named *Homo heidelbergensis* after a chinless lower jaw discovered in 1907 near Heidelberg, Germany. This species evolved from *Homo erectus* and looks much like its predecessor from the neck down, but the size and shape of the brain differ and its teeth are smaller. *Heidelbergensis* brains were about the size of ours and more like ours in shape, being higher above the ears than *erectus*, but still long and low compared with modern skulls (**23**). The term 'archaic humans' is often used to describe these descendants of *erectus* who are not quite modern humans.

Homo heidelbergensis is the immediate ancestor of the Neanderthal and by 300,000 bp some of the physical features which define Neanderthal had developed. They are clearly expressed in a remarkable collection of bones found at Atapuerca, central Spain. Near the Gran Dolina site described in the last chapter, another cave called 'The Pit of the Bones' (Sima de los Huesos), has provided palaeoanthropologists with a unique cross section of a community of archaic humans. More than 1,000 bones representing at least 30 individuals — men, women and children — have been excavated from a deep vertical shaft in the limestone. How the bodies got there is unclear but important. Perhaps the bodies were washed in naturally or dragged in by lions. Gnaw marks made by a large cat have been found on some of the bones. But the shaft is a steep 43ft (13m) drop and not a likely home for lions or any large predator. Alternatively, the dead were deliberately dumped into this shaft as part of some ritual disposal of bodies, making this the earliest evidence for deliberate burial.

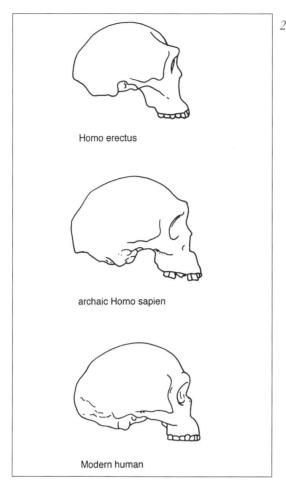

Homo erectus

archaic Homo sapien

Modern human

23   The skulls, in profile from top to bottom, of Homo erectus, Homo heidelbergensis *and* Homo sapiens.

Nothing about the archaeological record of *Homo erectus* suggests that the species recognised or responded to death as a significant event in the lives of individuals or communities. Atapuerca may be at the threshold of a new form of awareness or consciousness of others and their feelings. Some sense of empathy is necessary if humans are to construct guidelines for living based on moral principles — culture in other words. The recognition of death as a loss not just to a family but to a community is a potent sign that a human level of empathy exists. Burials, and especially burials with objects placed with the dead (**grave goods**), are considered by most archaeologists to be clear evidence of a kind of behaviour which is recognisably modern. The evidence from the bone pit at Atapuerca is tantalising but equivocal. There is no artificially made grave and there are no grave goods. Neanderthals did bury their dead, and very occasionally with objects. This aspect of their social life makes for an interesting comparison with their ancestor, *Homo heidelbergensis* and with rival modern humans.

The Atapuerca bones show a group of individuals whose physical features differ greatly. Some have a modern brain size but others less than modern.

24 *The face of a Neanderthal showing the heavy brow ridges, broad cheek bones and large nasal cavity typical of the species (after Brace 1971). This specimen is from Gibraltar, Spain, and was found in 1848.*

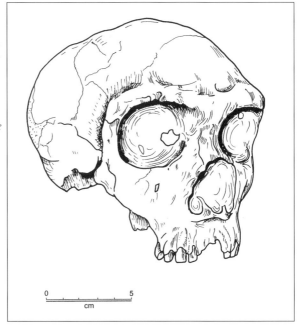

Then there are the features of the skull and skeleton which link some individuals more closely with Neanderthals than others. This is a population undergoing change, but one feature is consistent — size. By the time of the Atapuerca Pit of Bones, tall Boxgrove man had evolved into a compact European well suited to coping with a cold climate. A short stocky body has a relatively smaller surface area and this helps to conserve body heat and energy use. The tall tropical frame of *erectus* acted as a radiator to keep the body and especially the brain cool, a good design for the savannah but an inefficient one for the icy wastes of the tundra. (Some Arctic peoples today, such as the Inuit of Greenland, have the same compact body shape that evolved separately with archaic Europeans.)

Neanderthals carried on the trends started at Atapuerca. By 130,000 years ago, they had evolved a distinctive package of physical traits which set them apart from other archaic humans. Neanderthal limbs were short, giving their powerful bodies a stocky look. Their immense strength is a reminder that this species relied heavily on brawn as well as brain to survive. The Neanderthal face must have been a sight to behold with its large broad nose, big eyes, heavy brow ridges, low forehead and sweeping cheekbones (**24**). The lower jaw was also chinless, a feature inherited from *Homo erectus*. Neanderthal front teeth or incisors were large and often show heavy wear as if they were using their teeth as a third hand to hold objects. Their incisors also often have fine cut marks perpendicular to the length of the tooth, probably as a result of holding something like meat between the teeth and slicing off bits. This practice might have its roots at the time of Boxgrove where an incisor has been found with similar scratches and it has even been observed in more recent times among the Inuit.

25   Used pigments (hematite and limonite) from a 300,000 year old site in Zambia, Africa.

The large expanded face behind the cheeks and beneath the bony eyebrows of the Neanderthal held large cavities or sinuses. These sinuses along with the broad nose may have been adaptations to the cold. The large nose and sinuses may have helped to warm and moisten cold dry air before it reached the lungs. The large sinuses might also have insulated the temperature-sensitive brain from exposure to extreme cold. These are speculations but they highlight just how physically different Neanderthals were from *Homo sapiens*, differences which warrant placing Neanderthals in a separate species, *Homo neanderthalensis*.

Briefly returning to archaic humans outside Europe, in Africa *Homo heidelbergensis* developed along different lines from European archaics. The African descendants of *erectus* retained the tropical body shape but evolved a high rounded skull like ours with a prominent forehead (see **23**). The fossil record shows this happening between 200,000 and 130,000 years ago. DNA analyses of living humans also point to an African root for *Homo sapiens* evolving about 200,000 years ago. The archaeological record of Africa for this time is intriguing, it shows the emergence of new behaviours including the use of pigments and the making of complex tools. Lumps of red and yellow coloured minerals, called haematite and limonite, were being collected and brought to camp sites. The evidence comes from archaeological sites in Zambia and Kenya (**25**). The rocks were rubbed and scraped indicating that they had been used, but how and for what purposes? Maybe they were body paints used to decorate dancers taking part in communal rituals, to mark tools to show ownership or even used as medicines and preservatives. No

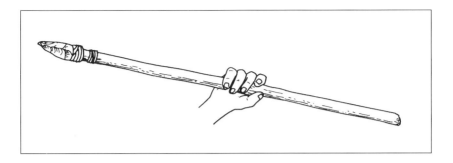

26   *A composite tool made of three parts: a shaped wooden shaft, a flaked-stone tip, a tendon binding and together they make a spear.*

unambiguous clues survive. Archaeologists must build — and test — their theories using the artefacts themselves, their associations with other artefacts and with examples of pigment-use drawn from living hunter-gatherers.

Perhaps the roots of what we recognise as art and ritual, two thoroughly modern behaviours, lie in these unpromising lumps of coloured rock. At the same time that pigment was being collected and rubbed a fundamental change in stone tool technology took place in Africa. The large, heavy handaxe was replaced by lightweight and complex tools made of flakes and long sharp blades (see Chapter 5), glued and bound into handles of wood or bone. These *composite* tools were not just easier to carry, they were a smart use of resources. An average handaxe consumes a large piece of stone, but a small flake in a handle can do the same jobs, at a fraction of the materials cost. In areas where good stone for knapping is scarce or inaccessible — such as in dense forests, on river floodplains or on Mendip — composite tool technology offers clear advantages. Lightweight, stone-tipped weapons are another and deadly benefit of composite technology (**26**) (see Chapter 5). These innovations must have eased life as a forager by making the search for food more predictable, a little less dangerous and by opening new environments for exploitation.

Composite technology also represents an intellectual advance as well as being immensely practical. Making a tool of multiple parts involves planning as does making a handaxe, but the difference is in the greater integration of different kinds of knowledge. A simple hafted knife might incorporate bone for the handle, flint for the working edge, and plant resin for the glue. Each material comes from a different source, has differing properties and must work together if the tool is to be successful. An intellectual threshold was crossed with the development of composite technology; the worlds of the organic and inorganic were combined for the first time. The foundation was laid for the complex technologies on which all modern humans depend.

Africa in the period between 400,000 and 200,000 years ago was a cauldron of change. Why this continent should be the centre of innovation and the evolution of the modern human form is a basic question for palaeo-anthropologists to tackle. For the time being there is simply not enough

51

known about this crucial period to begin to answer such a big question. Perhaps a combination of population growth and climate change spurred the development of a new species, new technology and new ways of behaving. Developing and testing these kind of speculations will keep the student of African prehistory busy for many years to come.

The Asian fossil record for the period after 500,000 BP is fascinating in its complexity. Something like *heidelbergensis* lived in China about 350,000 years alongside *Homo erectus*. The island of Java has very early evidence for *erectus* at 1.6 million years ago and also very late evidence of *erectus* living there less than 50,000 years ago. That is just yesterday in the reckoning of most palaeoanthropologists. If the more recent dates are confirmed then *Homo erectus* was not only a long-lived and successful species; it was not our direct ancestor and not the ancestor of modern south-east Asians. This is a significant piece of information in support of the Out of Africa theory and, as always, a source of controversy.

Neanderthals on the sidelines

In July 1997 a startling article appeared in the scientific journal *Cell* and made headlines world-wide. Fragments of genetic material known as **mitochrondial** DNA, which is passed on solely through the maternal line, had been unexpectedly found in the bones of a Neanderthal. This is the same kind of DNA that was extracted from Cheddar Man and used in the discovery of a living descendant (see Chapter 6 for a detailed discussion). The announcement by Matthias Kring and Svante Pääbo of the University of Munich startled the academic world on three accounts: the source of the DNA, its age and its implications for the fate of Neanderthals.

The DNA was extracted from an arm bone of the first skeleton recognised as Neanderthal. In using the original specimen, Pääbo and team removed any doubt about the identity of the skeleton. There is a poetic justice in returning to the first recognised human fossil to apply the latest in twentieth-century science. The bones were discovered in 1856 by quarry workers blasting a hillside along the Neander Valley, near Düsseldorf in northwestern Germany. Westbury Cave was not the first site to be found this way. The blast exposed a cave with fossil bones including limb bones and the top of a skull which looked distinctly different from living humans. The skull cap had prominent bony brow ridges arching over each eye and the shape of the skull was long and the forehead low. The limb bones were robust.

At the time of the Neander Valley discovery, Charles Darwin's *Origin of Species* (1859) was still being written. The concept that humans had evolved and once shared a common ancestor with chimps was unknown if not unthinkable. The story of how Neanderthal came to be accepted as a fossil human species is well known and well told by Chris Stringer and Clive Gamble (*In search of Neanderthals* 1993) and is not repeated here.

The Neanderthal DNA came from an individual who lived about 50,000 years ago. That was the second surprise — that DNA survived so long (see Chapter 6). Most importantly, the recovery of ancient Neanderthal DNA meant that for the first time a direct comparison could be made between them and us. The Out of Africa theory could be tested free of arguments based only on skeletal traits and interpretations of the archaeological record. If Neanderthals were the direct ancestors of living Europeans then the genes of the two groups should look similar. If on the other hand, Neanderthals made no real genetic contribution to modern Europeans — this would show up in a comparison of DNA — then they must have been replaced by another population and ultimately have become extinct.

Copies were made of the fragment of Neanderthal DNA using a technique called **polymerase chain reaction** (PCR). The development of PCR in the 1980s and refinements since have made the study of individual genes and even fragments of genes possible. This is an extraordinary feat in its own right but for our story the extraction and copying of *ancient* DNA is the real achievement. The fragments of Neanderthal DNA gleaned from the arm bone were copied many times to make a reference collection which was then checked for evidence of contamination, a real danger with ancient DNA, especially for bones handled in museums. A sample of the bone was sent for independent analysis to Pennsylvania State University and the American scientists also found the same distinctive stretch of Neanderthal DNA. The 'clean' copies were then compared against the same stretch of mitochondrial DNA in living humans and in chimpanzees. Comparisons were made with about 1,000 DNA samples representing modern Africans, Europeans, Asians, Native Americans, aboriginal Australians and Pacific islanders.

The results were conclusive: Neanderthals had made no genetic contribution to modern Europeans or to any other contemporary population. They were a separate extinct species (*Homo neanderthalensis*) and not simply a regional variant of us (*Homo sapiens neanderthalensis*). There were simply too many differences between the ancient Neanderthal DNA and ours to make them direct ancestors. The Out of Africa theory was vindicated, at least in Europe. The DNA evidence confirmed what many palaeonthropologists and archaeologists had long suspected, that Neanderthals were an evolutionary cul-de-sac.

The ancient DNA had another surprise in store. The Munich team estimated that the evolutionary split between Neanderthals and our last common ancestor — late *Homo erectus* or *Homo heidelbergensis* — took place about 600,000 years ago. This length of time was needed for all the genetic differences between us and Neanderthals to accumulate. Dating evolutionary events using a genetic clock is controversial (see p132) and in this case the DNA date for the Neanderthal split was older than the fossil and archaeological evidence. The skeletons from the Pit of Bones at Atapuerca, for example, showed that some Neanderthal traits were emerging about 300,000 years ago. The difference in age between the fossil bones and the DNA was narrowed in 1998 with the recovery of more DNA from the same Neanderthal bone. Pääbo and team doubled the amount of genetic material including new areas of the DNA which meant more detailed comparisons with modern populations could be made. The results confirmed the earlier conclusion that Neanderthals are not our ancestors but they also reduced the timing of the split to between 500,000 and 400,000 years ago. The agreement between the DNA date and the fossil dates was almost too good to be true.

We still have to be cautious. The Neanderthal DNA extracted by the Munich team comes from just one individual whose DNA might be atypical for the species with perhaps more variability than normal. In an ideal world, the analysis of DNA taken from other Neanderthals and even from early *Homo sapiens* would make for a stronger case and perhaps in time this will happen. But for the moment, all the various strands of evidence — genetic, skeletal and archaeological — place the origin of Neanderthals in the interval between the tall folk of Boxgrove and the stockier bodies which fill the Pit of Bones at Atapuerca. The earth had settled into the long rhythm of the climatic clock, ice age Europe provided the barrier and the stimulus for a new cold adapted species to evolve. European archaic humans were now isolated from their African and Asian brethren.

When the barrier was breached about 40,000 years ago, incoming *Homo sapiens* found a continent inhabited by not only a physically different species but one which behaved differently. The story of this alien encounter is charted in the archaeological record.

Brawn, brains and a touch of art

The archaeological record gives us evidence for the types of tools the human species made, their burial customs and art, the types of settlements they built and the way they made a living. By looking at this evidence we can see whether human species continued intact, were replaced or changed. By all these measures, a fundamental change in human behaviour took place across Europe between 40,000 and 30,000 BP. New types of stone and bone tools appear, burials become more elaborate, bone beads and cave art appear, camp sites are larger and more organised and hunting strategies become more successful and less risky. Archaeologists recognise this range of new behaviours as the beginning of the **Upper Palaeolithic**, a period which lasted in full from 40,000 to 10,000 years ago and which is the record of *Homo sapiens*. The Upper Palaeolithic overlapped by 10,000 years with the preceding long-lived **Middle Palaeolithic** which lasted from 300,000 to 30,000 years ago and is the time of the Neanderthals. The Middle Palaeolithic by comparison has a more limited range of stone tools and almost no bone tools. Cave art is absent, burials are simple, living sites are small and informal and hunting strategies for some Neanderthals, at least, are frankly dangerous.

The 10,000 years of overlap between the Upper and Middle periods is another litmus test for the Out of Africa theory. Some archaeologists see this as a period during which Neanderthals evolved both physically and behaviourally into modern humans. This is an argument for continuity. Others argue persuasively that the appearance of Upper Palaeolithic traits heralds the arrival of modern humans into Europe with new ideas. This is the argument for replacement. Both sides of the debate, and those who fall between the two extremes, accept the coexistence of Upper and Middle Palaeolithic technologies but cannot agree on its significance. The genetic and fossil evidence, when added to the equation, tip the balance in favour of the replacement model.

Recent studies of Neanderthal hunting strategies in Israel and Italy reinforce the image we have from their bones, of a species which lived a physically demanding lifestyle. Technology, social cooperation and language were all part of Neanderthal life but physical strength had an equally large role to play. Erik Trinkaus, an expert on Neanderthals, has studied the location and frequency of broken bones in a sample of complete Neanderthal skeletons. Most had suffered injuries to the upper body, neck and head; a pattern which is today common to rodeo riders. It seems that hunting was certainly confrontational with game probably killed by a stabbing spear which works best at close quarters. A similar study of Upper Palaeolithic skeletons has not been done but it might highlight the advantages of the more complex technologies and hunting strategies of modern humans. Physically, early modern humans were taller and more lightly built than Neanderthals, a legacy of our tropical origin. In a competition of brute strength Neanderthals would win but when it came to using the brain to solve problems *Homo sapiens* had the upper hand.

Notable innovations of the Upper Palaeolithic include basketry as shown by the recent discovery of woven fibre impressions on clay at the campsite of Dolni Vestonice, Czech Republic. Baskets for carrying and storing food and nets for trapping small animals were probably part of the successful strategy employed by modern humans in coping with ice age Europe. Other better-known technological fixes include well made hearths with stone linings which not only constrain the ashes but also retain heat. Fine bone needles also appear which could have been used to make tailored weatherproof clothing like the parka and boots made by the Inuit today. The use of bone and antler as raw materials for tool making is a hallmark of the Upper Palaeolithic and perhaps one of the most significant differences between ourselves and Neanderthals. As Cambridge archaeologist Paul Mellars observes, Upper Palaeolithic peoples appreciated the *plastic* properties of these materials — they could be shaped into a variety of tools and they are lightweight and resilient. The making of bone and ivory artefacts marks an important intellectual distinction between the two species and may reflect basic differences in the working of the brain.

In *A Prehistory of the Mind* (1996) archaeologist Stephen Mithen argues that Neanderthals perceived the world in a fundamentally different way from modern humans. The Neanderthal mind was organised into separate areas of specialised intelligence such as tool making, language and natural history knowledge which rarely worked together toward problem solving. The result was a limited capability to innovate, something seen in the limited range of stone tools made by Neanderthals. Modern humans by comparison have highly integrated minds which bring a range of intelligences to bear on problem solving with creative results. The variety of stone, bone and antler tools and their rapid development during the Upper Palaeolithic is a testimony to this creative explosion. But perhaps the most telling difference between us and Neanderthals is their lack of art.

But is it art?

What we think of as 'art' today involves symbols — a painting, sculpture or half a cow in formaldehyde — which convey various levels of meaning, some intended others not, depending on the viewer. Modern artists use a variety of materials and combinations to express their feelings about the world and to engage and even challenge the viewer to think about his or her role in society. In most small societies, like hunter-gatherers, 'art' does not exist as something separate but is part of daily life — tools, clothes and bodies might be decorated. This kind of art builds a sense of belonging to a group. The absence of art among Neanderthals may mean they did not have the strongly developed sense of a social group but, more importantly in terms of their minds, it says they did not make the intellectual leap necessary to use symbols to represent the world around them.

Symbols are the basis for communicating abstract ideas like next year, Mickey Mouse and beliefs in invisible beings such as gods. Neanderthals seem to have managed without them, or if they did talk about such things, Mickey Mouse aside, they did not leave many clues in the archaeological record. Modern humans used symbols consistently — we see this in their art — and though we will never know the meanings behind their art we can say that they had the capacity to transmit complex ideas, to create group identities and to plan for the future. The overall effect is to make for a more cohesive group with a strong sense of identity. This may have been an added advantage for a group of immigrants colonising a new world and one in which other humans — Neanderthals — were already living.

Was the replacement of Neanderthals by anatomically modern outsiders a rapid or gradual process? Looking at the archaeological record we can see a spread of modern humans from east to west (**27**). The earliest Upper Palaeolithic technology is found in the Middle East about 45,000 years ago, then in eastern Europe at 40,000 BP and about the same time in western Europe (Spain). By stone age reckoning that is rapid. But Neanderthals did not disappear instantly in the face of superior brains and technology. They lived alongside our ancestors for up to 10,000 years. In central France, at the site of Arcy sur Cure, the remains of a Neanderthal dated to 33,000 BP were found with stone and bone tools which look like a cross between Middle and Upper Palaeolithic technologies. Similar mixtures of technologies are found in central Europe and Italy. Perhaps Neanderthals borrowed a few ideas from modern humans, in particular bone and blade tools. Did the borrowing take place through face to face contact with moderns or did Neanderthals simply imitate the tools left behind at Upper Palaeolithic camps? Did the two groups get along so well that they exchanged mates or marriage partners as well as technology? A time machine would be useful.

The end of the line

The ancient DNA discovered by the Munich geneticists provides a powerful clue to the social relations between Neanderthals and modern humans —

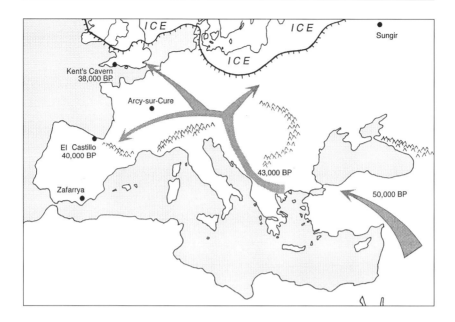

27   *Modern humans (*Homo sapiens) *spread from the Middle East into Europe
      starting about 50,000 BP, reaching Bulgaria by 43,000 BP, northern Spain
      by 40,000 BP and Britain soon after.*

they kept to themselves, at least when it came to mates. The Neanderthal
DNA differs so much from our own that we are clearly two distinct species,
and by definition that means a mating of the two could not produce viable
offspring. Neanderthals became extinct about 30,000 years ago. A last refuge
was found in southern Spain, at the site of Zafarrya near Malaga. Neanderthal
bones were discovered in a narrow passage in a limestone cliff face. These late
hangers on were still using Middle Palaeolithic tools with no outside
influences. The discovery is a poignant reflection of a species pushed to the
margins of its former range by another more successful competitor.

  In biological terms the demise of the Neanderthal is an example of the
principle of *competitive exclusion*. When two species compete for the same
limited resources one will triumph at the expense of the other. Modern
humans may have had a clear technological advantage — they simply
extracted more food from the environment for less effort and risk. Our
ancestors may have been more sociable as well. Trade links operated across
Europe in the Upper Palaeolithic with high quality flint from central Europe
being carried to the fringes of the continent and seashells from the Atlantic
and Mediterranean coasts brought far inland. Modern humans were in
contact with each other across large areas, exchanging information, gifts and
perhaps even mates. Social networks exist today among many hunter-
gatherers, especially those living in harsh environments. They act as an
insurance system against hard times. The striking cave art and beautifully
made carvings found in the Upper Palaeolithic may have been an integral part
of these social networks.

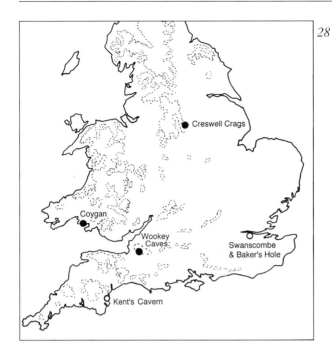

*28 Early (open
circle) and later
Neanderthal sites
in Britain.*

Neanderthals on the Mendips

We are still waiting for the discovery of classic Neanderthal bones in Britain. A tooth or toe would be a start, but until that day we must make do with two very early possible Neanderthals. The gravel terraces of the Thames River have proved a rich source of animal bones, stone artefacts and the occasional human fossil. It was here, at Swanscombe (**28**) that three pieces of a skull cap (minus the brow and face) were unearthed at different times, the first in 1935, the second in 1936 and the third in 1955. Amazingly the pieces fitted together showing they came from the same individual. This person who lived about 200,000 years ago had features on her skull — 'Swanscombe Man' seems to have been female — which are found in later Neanderthals. Swanscombe tells us that descendants of *Homo heidelbergensis* were adapting physically to the oscillating climate of glacial Europe.

In terms of behaviour, they were making handaxes like those found at Boxgrove 300,000 years earlier. At the nearby site of Bakers Hole, also along the Thames, a new way of making stone flakes entered the repertoire of these early Neanderthals. The **Levallois** technique is a set of strategies for making flakes of predictable size, shape and thickness (**29**). The technique is named after a chic Paris suburb where the characteristic cores and flakes were first recognised. The Levallois strategy of carefully shaping a core before striking off flakes was widespread across the world of archaic sapiens from Africa, across Europe and into western Asia. Its appearance and success coincides with the development of composite tool technology. In the world of Neanderthals, wooden spears like those of Schöningen and Clacton could be made even more effective with sharp stone tips. Other tools such as knives

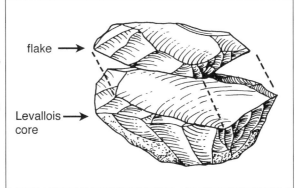

29   A Levallois core is carefully prepared by removing small flakes from the top, bottom and sides to create a domed surface from which large thin flakes are struck.

and saws would be easier (and safer) to hold and more effective at cutting when placed in handles. Just when and where the Levallois technique — and hafting — developed is uncertain but they may ultimately be of African origin. In the time of *Homo erectus*, a form of Levallois technique was used in southern Africa to produce large thin flakes for trimming into handaxes, long before archaic sapiens emerged.

Human bones and stone artefacts of about the same age as Swanscombe have been found in north Wales at the site of Pontnewydd Cave. Stephen Aldhouse-Green, formerly of the National Museum of Wales and now at University of Wales College, Newport, excavated twenty teeth from deposits about 220,000 years old. The size and shape of the dental roots are like those of later Neanderthals showing that the evolution of *Homo heidelbergensis* into a cold adapted European species was well underway. The stone tools — handaxes and Levallois flakes — are unusual in that they are made mostly of volcanic rocks such as rhyolite. Flint, the usual material for making stone tools, was in short supply around Pontnewydd. The inhabitants used what was commonly at hand and that was volcanic rock, transported to the vicinity of the cave by natural glacial action. Neanderthals' ancestors were resourceful even if they were limited in their ability to innovate.

After such a promising start the fossil record in Britain becomes quiet. No classic Neanderthal remains have been found. Their absence is not necessarily evidence of absence, it may simply be a matter of time before a discovery is made. Alternatively, the lack of bones may be telling us that Neanderthals did not range this far north very often or in great numbers. In fact, the archaeological record of Britain is strangely silent for the period of the last interglacial, from 127,000 to 117,000 years ago. What makes this period unusual is that it was warm — hippotamous, elephant (**30**) and tortoise ranged from Yorkshire to Trafalgar Square — and the landscape was forested but humans chose to avoid Britain. Maybe Neanderthals did not have the technology to cope with thick oak and elm forests. Their absence remains a mystery. Not until the climate changed and became colder with the start of the last glacial cycle did Neanderthals return. Their artefacts are found as far north as Creswell Crags in Derbyshire west into Wales at Coygan Cave, near Laugharne, and at Kent's Cavern, Torquay (see **28**).

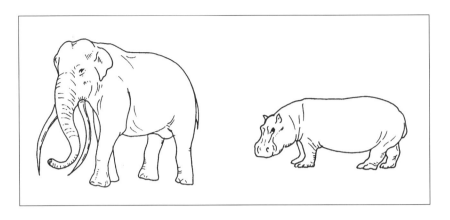

30   *The hippopotamus and the straight-tusked elephant (now extinct) lived in Britain 120,000 years ago during a warm interglacial period.*

A review of environmental and archaeological data by Roger Jacobi and Andy Currant of the Natural History Museum reveals that Neanderthals were rarely around before 60,000 years ago. Such a late arrival and early departure — by 30,000 BP at the latest — means Neanderthals had only a relatively short time in which to leave their mark. This and their small numbers may explain why we find just a trace of this extinct species in the caves of southern Britain.

We know that Neanderthals lived on and around the Mendips from isolated cave and surface finds of a distinctive small pear or triangular-shaped handaxe with a flat base, also called a *bout coupé* handaxe (**31**). Similar tools are known from Neanderthal sites in western Europe, especially in France. But where a Neanderthal presence is most strongly felt on Mendip is on the southern slopes near the show cave of Wookey Hole.

A threesome: Hyaena Den, Badger Hole and Rhinoceros Hole

These intriguingly named caves lie on the east side of a steep ravine opposite the entrance to Wookey Hole (**32**). The river Axe emerges at the head of the ravine and feeds a Victorian canal which supplies the old paper mill at Wookey. Together, these two water courses isolate the caves from public view. The caves today are protected monuments in recognition of their importance as the ancient campsites of Neanderthals, as the dens of extinct animals and, later, as shelters used by some of the first modern humans to arrive in Britain. Hyaena Den was discovered during the building of the canal and has been excavated at various times since 1859. It takes its name from the spotted hyaena which once made the cave home. Likewise, Rhinoceros Hole is named after the extinct woolly rhinoceros whose remains are found in the cave, along with horse and hyaena. Above Hyaena Den is Badger Hole, the largest of the three shelters and one still plagued by badgers today. Rhinoceros Hole and Badger Hole were investigated first by H.E. Balch early in the

31 *A triangular* bout coupé *handaxe from Badger Hole, Somerset.*

twentieth century and have been the sites of more recent scientific excavation.

The earliest excavations in the ravine were carried out by William Boyd Dawkins, a geologist with an interest in archaeology. His work at Hyaena Den in the 1850s took place at a time when the idea of human prehistory was new. Charles Darwin had just published the *Origin of Species* in 1859 and discoveries of stone tools with the bones of extinct animals were still viewed with scepticism by believers in the strict Biblical account of creation. Excavations by Boyd Dawkins on the Mendips and elsewhere in Britain helped consolidate the fledgling discipline of Palaeolithic archaeology by confirming the Stone Age antiquity of humans. At Hyaena Den he found layers of hyaena droppings — they are distinctively white — alternating with layers of stone tools and hearths. Hyaenas and Neanderthals took turns living in the cave. Boyd Dawkins was particularly thorough at Hyaena Den, leaving very little of the cave unexcavated. Archaeologists today are aware that methods of excavation, dating and environmental analysis are constantly improving. Caves are a finite resource and archaeology is by its very nature destructive. Before excavating any cave the archaeologist must have a research strategy which justifies the need to dig and one which includes preserving intact deposits for future generations of researchers and for the public to whom the past belongs.

Despite the nearly complete excavation of Hyaena Den, modern researchers have been able to glean more information about the prehistory of the cave through careful analysis of surviving deposits. This has included work by the University of Bristol Spaeleological Society and archaeologist Roger Jacobi. Together with volunteers, they have discovered surviving deposits beneath the entrance and remnants clinging to the roof. Techniques of recovering artefacts have improved greatly since Hyaena Den was first

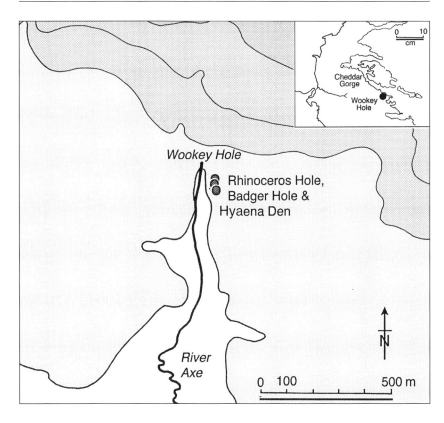

32   The Wookey cave sites of Hyaena Den, Badger Hole and Rhinoceros Hole were used by Neanderthals and by Homo sapiens.

explored with the 3-dimensional recording of artefacts and the use of fine mesh sieves now routine. The most recent excavations have found subtle traces of prehistoric occupation in the mouth of the cave. Scattered chips of flint from stone tool making were discovered with cut and burnt fragments of animal bone. These are the kinds of uninspiring artefacts which are the bread and butter of archaeologists who try to piece together past human behaviour. The *context* of finds, that is where they are found and with which other artefacts, is just as important as the artefacts themselves.

Eleven small handaxes were found by Boyd Dawkins at Hyaena Den, including one complete and one broken *bout coupé* handaxe, and flakes from shaping the handaxes. But there is much more to the site than a few traces of Neanderthal technology, the cave also held animal bones. The spotted hyaena which gives the cave its name was a great collector of animal bone from its forays as a scavenger and hunter. Hyaenas today raise their pups in caves and rock shelters where the floors are strewn with half chewed bone and faeces white with calcium. Prehistoric hyaenas seem to have shared their modern descendants' habit of accumulating bone in dens and these collections provide a valuable source of fossils for the palaeontologist. The animal bones

33 *Typical animals found on and around the Mendip hills in the time of Neanderthals, about 60,000 to 30,000 years ago. They include from left to right, top to bottom: woolly mammoth, cave lion, bear, spotted hyaena, horse, woolly rhinoceros, reindeer and bison. (after barton 1997)*

from Hyaena Den, Rhinoceros Hole and other sites in Britain give a glimpse of the type of landscape in which Neanderthals lived. It was a cold, dry open grassland which supported woolly mammoth, woolly rhinoceros, horse, reindeer, bear, cave lion, wolf and, of course, spotted hyaena (**33**). This 'mammoth-steppe' ranged from Britain eastwards across northern Europe and into Siberia and has been dated to a period from 60,000 to about 25,000 years ago. Neanderthals would disappear from this barren landscape long before the mammoth became extinct.

Back at the office, I think what a long time it is since I heard from Bryan Sykes. I call him. 'DNA, what DNA?' he asks. 'The DNA I asked you to get,' I said. 'In my fax.' 'Fax, what fax?' he asks. 'I'm still waiting for you to give the go-ahead.' I groan. The fax that disappeared into electronic thin air between Ireland and Oxford. It had to be this one. Films are full of false starts, maybe this was going to be one of them. I am conscious of my timetable. We are scheduled to start cutting the films in January. Will there be time to get the DNA from Cheddar Man, process it, collect samples from Cheddar, process them? Film it all? Can I afford it? I am already overshot and overspent on the film. 'Well, if you can get the jaw to me immediately, maybe we can do it,' is Bryan's suggestion. Talk to Chris Stringer.

I talk to Chris Stringer. I know he won't let the jaw out of his sight, so I can't volunteer to take it from London to Oxford myself. Chris is pessimistic. He is very busy; he won't be able to make a special journey to Oxford with the jaw, but he will be going to a conference there at the end of January 1997. He will take it then, if that is not too late for the programme schedule. I promise to let him know before the conference date.

January comes. January is almost gone. I consult our timetable for the film. No time now to process ancient material from the jaw of Cheddar Man. No time to test local residents if I am to keep to my editing schedule. I think of the budget. I decide, regretfully, and wishing I had a bigger budget and no hard choices to make, to abandon the DNA. It is the end of the story.

I fax Bryan Sykes and Chris Stringer accordingly. Bryan is on the phone the next day. 'I've already done it,' he says. 'Drilled the tooth, got a result, a very clear profile.' He sounds quite matter of fact. 'Aren't you excited about it,' I asked him. 'Yes,' he said, 'I am. It is very exciting.' 'What a shame,' I said, 'we shan't be able to do the rest.' Bryan is not pleased: 'Go to all this trouble. Say you don't want it.' I say I will call him back tomorrow. I talk to Harvey. I talk to Tom Archer at HTV who offers encouragement but no cash. I do more sums. Call Bryan the next day. Please come and do the tests in Cheddar. We talk about the best way to compose a sample; he suggests doing sixth-formers in a local school. That is what they have done elsewhere. That seems like a good idea; it will fit nicely with the other filming we have done at the school. And, I suggest, it will add some more cases to Bryan's national DNA survey. I am keen on this aspect of the project. Television is often parasitic on other peoples' research — here was a chance to make a contribution in the other direction.

> *Late January 1997* Philip P. phoned to say he would like to come back to school in the near future and do some more filming. Apparently a scientific team have managed to take a sample of DNA from 'Cheddar Man', the 9000-year-old skeleton found in the caves in 1903. 'You have heard of him?' 'Yes, of course, — but I don't know much more! Philip explains that he would like to bring the DNA team to Cheddar and film them taking some samples from local people to see if anyone might be related to Cheddar Man'. Could I

get some of our students whose families have lived in the area for generations and ask them if they would be willing to take part? Secondly, would some of our Year 9s be prepared to enact some scenes from Anglo-Saxon life to go with the Saxon Palace part of the programme? Tell him that on both counts there should be no problem in getting volunteers!
Adrian Targett

I spoke to Adrian Targett, Head of History, and asked about testing some of the students; perhaps some of the ones who have already been filmed for the programme. He thought about it, and said he needed a piece of paper to send to parents explaining the procedure and the uses to which the results might be put. I draft a letter and Adrian sends it to the parents of the selected students together with a consent form for them to sign, and Bryan Sykes' information sheet about his national survey.

Friday 7 February 1997 Emilçe Vega and her colleague, both of them colleagues of Bryan, arrive from Oxford to take DNA samples from people in the school. Thirteen students take part plus some adults. I have invited Mark Hill, member of an old-established Cheddar family, a former pupil taking time off from stacking shelves at Budgen's supermarket round the corner; Mrs Lane from the Manor House that adjoins the school — also with a long Cheddar pedigree. Vince Russett the archaeologist is there — without his mum. Mick joins in. Bob Smart from the Showcaves shows up to do his bit. 'They say curators get to look like their exhibits,' he mutters in his droll way, lining up with the other hopefuls, and looking more like a caricature of himself than anyone else.

> *Friday 7 February* Return of the film crew plus two scientists from Oxford. One of the scientists, a stunningly attractive young lady explains the science behind the procedure and what the procedure itself involves — the taking of a few cells from the inside of the mouth with what can best be described as a very short bristled toothbrush. The boys in the sample group hang on her every word — or rather they don't take their eyes off her! I am near the back of the line: one of the boys thought that the sampling would involve a blood sample taken with a giant hypodermic syringe so I told him it was nothing of the sort and that I'd have a sample taken to prove it was simple and painless. *Adrian Targett*

John Podpadec is doing the camera-work today. He sweeps up and down in front of the queue of DNA donors. Mick walks along behind the queue addressing camera as he goes and introducing what we are doing. Emilçe gives everyone a little flossing brush and shows them how to scrub the inside of the cheek to accumulate cell tissue for analysis. Some people do it with their mouths open. Some do it through pursed lips. As each person reaches the head of the line the scrubbed brushes are sealed in separate polythene bags, each labelled with the name of the donor, and placed carefully in Emilçe's black bag.

When it is all over, I am not all that optimistic — the chance of finding a direct descendant of Cheddar Man after all these years seems quite remote. I hope for the best and prepare for something less. The next week I call Bryan Sykes to see how things are coming along. Fine, he says. But on reflection he has decided not to tell me the name of anyone who might prove to be related to Cheddar Man. He tells me how not so long ago he did tests on an Irish woman who proved to be a direct descendant of Ice Man — the famous Alpine mummy — and she had been badgered for weeks by press calls from as far away as Japan. He was loath to inflict the pressure of such publicity onto a school student. I cannot disguise my alarm. The whole point of commissioning this research, and going into the red on the programme budget, is precisely to make such an identification — if one is there to be made. Why else does Bryan think I am going to pay him to do this work? 'Do the parents know about what they are letting their children in for?' he wants to know. They all had a letter, I explain.

I talk to Adrian Targett on the phone. He is convinced that parents are aware of what the testing is for and what its consequences might be in terms of publicity. We discuss how to handle matters if one of the students turns out to be related to CM. I fax the text of my letter and the consent form which all the parents have signed to Bryan in Oxford.

Monday 17 February 1997 From the Print Rooms in Bristol, where I am editing the programme, I fax Adrian a hand-written note. At the bottom of the page I say when we are hoping to have the results. 'It could be you,' I conclude in jest.

Colette Hodges is editing the Cheddar programme with me, neither of us knowing how it will end. I am very keen to emphasize the otherness of the Gorge and the strangeness — to our eyes — of the life that was led there by Neolithic peoples. One of the findings reported in a scientific paper co-authored by Bryan Sykes was that mitochondrial DNA collected from Basque people in Spain appeared to be the original European material. The linguistic oddity of the Basque language — completely unrelated to Indo-European tongues — somehow suggested it was an eccentric survival, or an exotic incursion from elsewhere in the world. The DNA evidence suggested the opposite — that the Basques were here first and the rest of us are interlopers. If Basques are the original Europeans, I thought, it would be good to use their music in the film. I found a CD of Basque music, entitled 'Lezao', and recorded by Tomás San Miguel with *Txalaparta*. To begin with I thought this must be the name of his group, but it is in fact both a kind of rhythm and a traditional Basque instrument, originally planks of wood laid on baskets and struck with wooden hammers. It sounds like horses' hoof-beats. In the track called 'Latidos' (heartbeats) the percussion of the *txalaparta* is accompanied by plaintive calls from the *alboka* a double reed instrument. Colette edits with a strong sense of atmosphere and she made haunting sequences that combined this music with pictures of the Gorge, minimally re-created stone age activity, and the bones of Cheddar Man. Later, when I re-read the sleeve notes I found that Lezao is the name of a cave near Tomás San Miguel's family home, and a place of mystery and imagination. Later still I learned that Tomás is the brother of a friend of the son of the man who taught me to make films.

Europe is a small place.

4 The moderns arrive

Humans the world over have a frightening capacity for creating enemies for the most trivial of reasons. Our readiness to see an 'us and them' on the basis of appearance, beliefs, language, customs, affiliation (especially football team) makes it relatively easy to imagine how our ancestors — anatomically modern humans — reacted when they first encountered Neanderthals. As modern humans moved into Europe about 40,000 years ago they could not have failed to notice the presence of another human species. Neanderthals as the indigenous population already knew well the lay of the land: the location of caves and shelters, sources of flint, the migration routes of animals, the rhythm of the seasons — in other words, how to cope with a glacial world. Perhaps it is a coincidence, but modern humans with their ancestral roots in the tropics first move into Europe from the Middle East during an interstadial or warm phase of the last glacial cycle.

Homo sapiens and Neanderthals were probably already aware of each other's existence. The caves of the eastern Mediterranean area, known as the Levant, hold the bone and stone artefacts of both species (**34**). Modern humans and Neanderthals were both using the area on and off for tens of thousands of years. They buried their dead in the caves, they lived in the caves and made very similar tools. It is hard to imagine the two groups living side by side for so long without competing with each other. Instead they may have moved in and out of the area with fluctuations in the climate — Neanderthals using the caves during cold phases and modern humans during warmer periods. For Neanderthals it was the southern limit of their range and for moderns the northern limit. This alternating use of the Levant lasted a long 50,000 years or so; it seems that *Homo sapiens* was in no hurry to enter ice age Europe. It took a warm phase and some new developments in technology to make the mountains and tundra liveable for our tropical ancestors.

By 40,000 years ago, modern humans had developed an efficient and adaptable technology of stone and bone tools which allowed them to adapt to almost any environment. They may have brought with them a tradition of extended social networks or alliances which gave moderns an advantage in coping with environmental uncertainty. They also may have brought with them a tradition of rituals including the use of paints to decorate themselves and their surroundings. As discussed in Chapter 3, art and ritual help to create a feeling of belonging to a larger group. This sense of belonging is part of dividing the world into 'us and them'. It is also part of creating rivals and

34   Homo sapiens and Neanderthals used the caves of the Middle East between 120,000 and 60,000 years ago as camp sites and burial grounds. The skull of a modern human from the site of Skhul in Israel (left, a cast) is higher and more rounded compared to a classic western European Neanderthal skull (right, cast).

justifying behaving aggressively towards them. Neanderthals who looked different and certainly behaved differently with their own traditions, customs and dialects would be 'them'.

An 'us and them' attitude emphasises differences and would be effective in building barriers between our ancestors and Neanderthals. Social mixing and the exchange of mates seem unlikely between two such very different groups of humans. The genetic evidence of Neanderthal DNA confirms that there was no or very little mixing. There is also no archaeological evidence for fighting between modern humans and Neanderthals, but our ancestors were very successful and very quickly moved from east to west. Upper Palaeolithic technology is found in northern Spain about 40,000 years ago, just two or three thousand years after appearing in Bulgaria in eastern Europe. Such a rapid move westward must have caused some tensions with the indigenous Neanderthal communities.

Their success may never have brought them into serious conflict with Neanderthals. Ezra Zubrow, a palaeodemographer, has calculated that modern humans needed to be only slightly more successful than Neanderthals in the search for food to become dominant. Within a few thousand years of their arrival modern humans grew in number at the expense of Neanderthals and pushed them toward extinction. The combination of an adaptable technology and long distance alliance networks

35 Important early and later Upper Palaeolithic cave sites in Britain.

could explain our ancestors' relatively rapid success. Within ten thousand years of entering Europe, modern humans had pushed the indigenous Neanderthals to the very edges of the continent. The small Spanish cave of Zafarrya is a vivid reminder of the fate of a once widespread species now reduced to a toehold and soon to be gone forever. Thirty thousand years ago, with Neanderthals on the verge of extinction in southern Europe modern humans were thriving on the northern fringes of the continent — Britain. These were the ancestors of Cheddar Man.

The early moderns in Britain

South-western Britain, including the Mendips, has several caves and sites in the open used by early modern humans as they settled in this new landscape (**35**). The most important of these are Kent's Cavern in Torquay and Paviland Cave on the Gower peninsula of south Wales. Both caves were used for burials and have been dated. On Mendip, early modern humans settled at Soldier's Hole in Cheddar Gorge and at Badger Hole near the modern show cave of Wookey Hole. At both locations they left their distinctive stone artefacts. The flint and bone artefacts found at these four sites belong to the early Upper Palaeolithic of Britain which lasted from 38,000 to about 20,000 years ago when the climate became too cold and dry for animals and humans. Both returned to Britain about 12,500 years ago when the climate improved. These late Upper Palaeolithic (12,500-10,000 BP) hunter-gatherers brought with them new kinds of tools and we find them in Gough's Cave.

Further south in Spain and France modern humans lived without interruption and the archaeological record is more complex. Archaeologists in these areas work with a sequence of Upper Palaeolithic cultures (Aurignacian, Gravettian, Solutrean, Magdalenian) with fine sub-divisions or phases of each. The continental sequence is based on hundreds of sites and hundreds of thousands of artefacts. Britain, by contrast, has just a few sites and a few thousand artefacts for the Upper Palaeolithic. This can be explained partly by the small number of hunter-gatherers living so far north and partly by the destructive effects of the ice age climate. The movement of ice sheets obliterates most traces of living sites on the ground surface. The seasonal freezing and thawing of the tundra surface also churns the soil, causing sites to be hopelessly mixed as the ground cracks open and then swells shut. On hill slopes, half-frozen sediments can form a liquid slush which slides downwards, either burying living sites below or transporting artefacts far from their original resting places. Caves then are the best sites for reconstructing the sequence of human occupation in Britain but as we have seen, often they too are disturbed by the likes of bears, hyaenas and us.

Kent's Cavern

Torquay today styles itself as the 'English Riviera' but at the time modern humans were arriving the area was anything but balmy. On the outskirts of the city is the famous show cave of Kent's Cavern. In the 1820s excavations by a priest, Father J. MacEnery, produced flint artefacts with the bones of extinct animals sealed beneath a thick layer of cave flowstone or stalagmite. The human presence was undoubtedly prehistoric and older than the Great Flood of the Old Testament. In the days before Darwin and the acceptance of evolution, this discovery was tantamount to heresy. That a priest should be the instigator was doubly embarrassing. Later excavations proved him right. William Pengelly between 1865 and 1880 undertook the first systematic excavation of Kent's Cavern and did so on behalf of the British Association for the Advancement of Science — archaeology had come of age. Pengelly confirmed what MacEnery had surmised: prehistoric humans were the contemporaries of now extinct animals. Kent's Cavern became and remains one of the most important archaeological sites in Britain.

The stalagmite deposit which sealed the flints and bones has now been dated by a technique called uranium-series (see Appendix) and has proved to be very old indeed, more than 350,000 years. The flints tools are handaxes and were left by the predecessors of Neanderthals. Neanderthals also used the cave, leaving behind their tools, especially the flat-based (*bout coupé*) handaxes. With such a long history of human use it is hardly surprising that *Homo sapiens* also made Kent's Cavern their home and burial place. Human bones were found by Pengelly and one of *Homo sapiens* has since been dated to 31,000 BP using an advanced form of radiocarbon dating known as accelerator mass spectrometry (AMS) dating. The technique has the great advantage over conventional radiocarbon dating in that only very small amounts of organic material — bone in this case — are needed to produce accurate dates. The Kent's Cavern date makes this probable burial one of the earliest in northern Europe.

36 *Stone spear points like this were made 30,000 years ago by Upper Palaeolithic hunter-gatherers across northern Europe. This example was found at Soldier's Hole, near Gough's Cave (after Campbell 1977).*

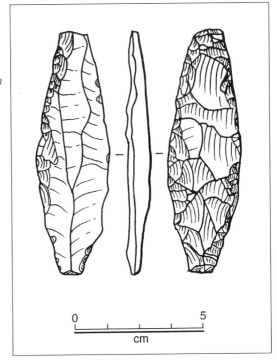

The Mendips

Not far from Gough's Cave on the south side of Cheddar Gorge is a small overhang or shelter called Soldier's Hole which was excavated in the 1920s. The site is important for its early Upper Palaeolithic artefacts and for the fact that these are beneath later Upper Palaeolithic artefacts. The most distinctive early artefacts are large spear points which have been flaked on both sides to make them thin and sharp (**36**). The points are made from **blades** which are long flakes with parallel edges that are struck from specially prepared blade cores. Tools made on blades are usually associated with the Upper Palaeolithic which means blade technology is largely the work of modern humans. The success of *Homo sapiens* in coping with the European environment was partly based on our ancestors' adaptable and efficient blade technology. Because blades are similar in size and shape they can be used as interchangeable parts of hafted tools. Put end to end in a handle, blades make a long and sharp cutting edge. If part of the edge breaks or becomes blunt then a new blade can be fitted and there is no need to make a new handle. A modern razor with its replaceable razor blades operates on the same principle.

Blades can also be turned into other standardised tool types for scraping hides and whittling wood. They can also be blunted to form a chisel-like cutting edge, or burins, which are tools for engraving bone and antler (**37**) and working softer stone. Other blade-based tools include borers and awls for drilling and piercing. These are just some of the tasks for which blades were used and they illustrate just how adaptable this technology could be. A spin-

71

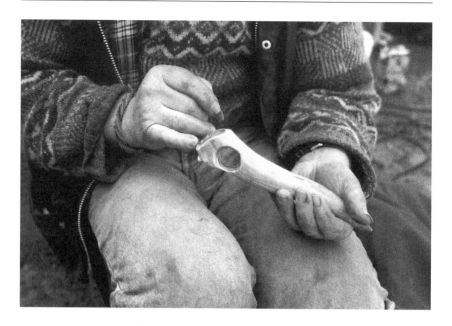

37   A flint engraving tool (burin) made on a blade and being used by Phil Harding to shape an antler bâton.

off of using standardised working bits in hafted tools is that time could be invested in making and *decorating* the handle. Handles now offer a new surface for humans to mark and express their personal or group identity.

The spear points found at Soldier's Hole are similar to points from the early Upper Palaeolithic deposits at Kent's Cavern and at Badger Hole, near the Hyaena Den at Wookey Hole. These three sites and others in Britain are part of widespread north European tradition of making carefully shaped spearpoints. They are found in Poland and further east in Russia between 43,000 and 35,000 years ago. Perhaps these spears were especially designed for hunting large game in an open landscape. The grasslands of 30,000 years ago were home to mammoth, woolly rhinoceros, giant deer and horse. Predators including lion, bear and spotted hyaena might also have inspired our ancestors to make stout stone-tipped spears.

Paviland Cave

Across the Bristol Channel, 70 miles (112km) to the west of Soldier's Hole as the arctic tern flies, is the well-known cave of Paviland (see **35**). Paviland Cave today is at the southern end of the Gower Peninsula, it is accessible at low tide and involves a steep climb up a craggy rock face (**38**). Thirty thousand years ago when the cave was used by modern humans the sea was far to the south and mammoth and horse grazed in the valley below. The cave is famous today for the burial of the 'Red Lady' of Paviland, an elaborate burial excavated early last century by the Rev. William Buckland, a geologist

38 The view from inside Paviland Cave (Wales) looking out across the Bristol Channel. Thirty thousand years ago the cave would have looked onto a grassy plain filled with herds of horse and bison.

as well as clergyman. Buckland's excavation in 1822 — like MacEnery's at Kent's Cavern — took place before the idea of a stone age past was acceptable. The burial with its mammoth ivory wands and bracelets, seashell beads and a liberal covering of haematite (red ochre) must have posed an intellectual challenge for the Rev. Buckland. Here was the body of a prehistoric human of some obvious antiquity but the prevailing interpretation of the Bible did not allow for such a find. Buckland resolved the dilemma by making the 'Red Lady' a Roman subject.

We know today that the she was a he, an adult male aged about 25, approximately 5ft 6in (1.7m) tall, who died 26,000 years ago. The elaborate burial ritual with its grave goods and covering of pigment could mean that the person buried was someone of importance or status in his community. Archaeologists know that often a person's social standing in life is reflected in death. This line of reasoning is discussed in more detail in the next chapter. For the moment, the tomb of Tutankhamun is just one spectacular example, in this case a head of state who was buried with luxury items appropriate to his position in Egyptian society and according to their beliefs in an afterlife. Just what the Paviland man may have done to warrant his elaborate send-off we will never know. A society of hunter-gatherers has far fewer roles and positions of influence for an individual than an Egyptian kingdom. Perhaps he was valued as a spiritual healer who intervened with the supernatural on behalf of his people or maybe he was an able hunter or a wise storyteller. We can only guess.

Paviland Cave was not just a burial ground but also a much used living site. A spear point like those from Badger's Hole, Soldier's Hole and Kent's Cavern tells us that the early Upper Palaeolithic people were possibly here by 35,000 BP. Artefacts belonging to another early phase dating to about 30,000 BP were also found and these have parallels with stone tools made in France and Spain at this time. It seems that ideas, if not people, moved long distances and quickly. Paviland was abandoned during the coldest phase of the last glacial cycle around 20,000 years ago and then re-occupied about 12,500 years ago. This was the same time that Gough's Cave was also being used by the direct ancestors of Cheddar Man.

Buckland's excavations removed most of the contents of Paviland Cave, but excavations in 1997 directed by Stephen Aldhouse-Green have shown that the surviving remnants of deposit still have much to offer. Modern scientific dating and environmental analyses will refine further the age of the site and allow a fuller reconstruction of the world in which Paviland man lived and died. Cave sites in Britain are rare and most have been excavated by earlier generations of archaeologists to the standards of their day. There is still much to be learned from these 'old' sites using new techniques and they deserve our care and respect.

The late Upper Palaeolithic at Gough's Cave

The principal attraction in Cheddar today is Gough's Cave. The archaeological record tells us that this large opening in the south side of the Gorge was also the main attraction 12,500 years ago (**39**). Most of what we know about the prehistory of the site comes from various alterations to the cave entrance to make it more accessible to visitors. A sad photograph taken of Cheddar Man shortly after his accidental discovery in 1903 shows a jumble of bones with the Gough brothers standing on either side, beaming with pride. Today, such a burial — and it probably was a burial — would be carefully recorded in three dimensions and maybe even lifted intact and excavated under laboratory conditions. This kind of detailed spatial information is essential for detecting whether the body was placed in a grave and with which grave goods, if any. By recording the location of artefacts, hearths and burials in caves, archaeologists can sometimes reconstruct general patterns of use. We know, for example, that people rarely lived beyond the reach of daylight in caves. Activities like making tools and preparing food often took place outside the cave or under the protection of an overhanging roof. Just inside the entrance itself makes a good sleeping area which can be made safe from roving animals and intruders. Such insights into the lives of Cheddar Man and his ancestors have been lost in the need to develop the cave as an attraction.

By the 1920s, the ever-growing tourist numbers meant a further widening

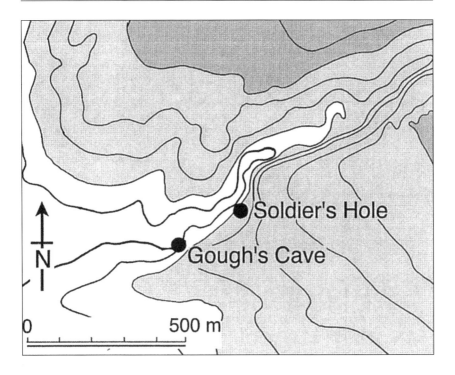

39   Gough's Cave and Soldier's Hole on the southeast side of Cheddar Gorge were used by Upper Palaeolithic hunter-gatherers.

of the entrance area was needed. The floor was to be dropped and levelled. The deposits were lowered along both walls of the entrance during excavations supervised and recorded by archaeologist R.F. Parry who was working on behalf of the Marquis of Bath. The bones of two adults and one child were recovered along with 7,000 flint artefacts and many animal bones. The flints represent the largest single collection of late Upper Palaeolithic artefacts found in Britain. The humans have since been radiocarbon dated (AMS) to between 12,400 and 11,800 BP. The time span falls nicely within the late Upper Palaeolithic.

A partial skull of an adult male is the more complete of the adults. Analysis of its size and shape by Chris Stringer of the Natural History Museum shows a clear resemblance to Cheddar Man who lived 3,000 years later. The other adult bone is a large lower jaw or mandible. This jaw is particularly intriguing because of the fine cuts and grooves on both the outside and inside surfaces. Some of these cuts may have been made by a flint knife. Perhaps someone cut the jaw free from the skull after death to remove the tongue, but why?

Cannibals?

Cannibalism is the act of eating human flesh. The word raises Hollywood images from Tarzan films of men in pith helmets being stewed alive in a large pot over a fire, surrounded by frenzied natives waiting for a taste. The racist overtones are part of the taint associated with the term. We think of humans who eat their own kind as little better than animals, but cannibals have had a bad press. In truth there are few *reliable* reports of cannibalism. Tales told by early European travellers in the Americas, Africa and Asia were distorted by colonial interests in making indigenous peoples seem less than human and needing civilising. These early accounts ignored possible motives for cannibalism other than pure savagery. Motives aside, anthropologist William Arens, of State University of New York at Stony Brook, surveyed historical and archaeological claims for cannibalism and concluded that very few could be verified. Arens' research was published in 1979 and since then the weight of academic opinion has been set against prehistoric anthropophagy (the technical term for cannibalism). Behind the scenes there has also been a strong element of political correctness in avoiding branding another's ancestors as savages. Archaeologists are scientists but they are also part of a wider society, they share its values and are sometimes blinded by them.

Before looking more closely at the evidence from Gough's Cave, it is worth considering the motives which might lead people to eat each other. Hunger, ritual and terror are the big three. Deciding which is acceptable and which is not is a matter of taste or morality. Under extreme conditions of starvation, people have resorted to cannibalism. This century has produced some well-known examples which need not be repeated here. Such acts of desperation must be distinguished from the ritual consumption of human remains. Reverence for the dead has many expressions today and in the past included eating human flesh and blood. Eating a piece of the dearly departed may be part of a private act of homage or part of public ritual. The most famous example in anthropological circles comes from the highlands of New Guinea where the brains of deceased relatives were eaten out of respect. The Aztec of central Mexico offered human sacrifices to their gods and ate the flesh of sacrificial victims who had been dressed to impersonate the gods. This was an act of divine communion but technically cannibalism. Closer to home, the invitation Christ gave to his apostles at the Last Supper to symbolically eat his body and drink his blood is recreated daily in Christian churches everywhere.

Cannibalism may also be an act of terror inflicted by an aggressor on enemies and used to build a fearsome reputation. Tim White, a palaeoanthropologist at the University of California, Berkeley, has found clear evidence for the deliberate butchering of adults and children at an 800-year-old site in the American Southwest. Cut marks on the bones were left from stripping the flesh, long bones were smashed to get at the marrow, then cooked in pots, and finally their heads were cut off and roasted. White even identified a 'pot polish' on the ends of thigh and arm bone fragments from being stirred in cooking pots. Human bones were treated just like the bones of other animals eaten at these sites. White concludes that cannibalism was used as part of a reign of terror between warring tribes with victims captured during raids and systematically slaughtered. Was this an act of vengeance, a respectful rite of ancestor veneration or just a meal?

Speaking of tongues

We can ask the same question of the 12,000-year-old jaw from Cheddar. The answer is uncertain except hunger seems the lesser motive. The remains of systematically cut, broken and smashed bones of horse, red deer, aurochs and arctic hare were found in the same deposits as the human bones at Gough's Cave. Starvation for such experienced hunter-gatherers as these seems unlikely. Perhaps they were practising an act of veneration. In this case the removing of the jaw and tongue would be a variation among the range of Upper Palaeolithic funerary rituals which ran the gamut from the very elaborate at Paviland with its grave offerings to a simple eating a piece of the departed at Cheddar. Alternatively, we may be distant witnesses to a violent event in which the occupants of the cave were attacked, killed and butchered by a rival group of hunter-gatherers. It is a dramatic story but one without much support.

The jaw from Parry's excavations has remained an anomaly as a sample of one, hardly the basis for reconstructing ancient rituals or acts of vengeance. Excavations at Gough's Cave in 1986-7 radically changed the picture. The excavation was undertaken by a team from the University of Lancaster (Roger Jacobi) and the British Museum (Chris Stringer and Andy Currant) to collect material from an area that was at risk from erosion especially during winter flooding. A small rectangle about 1.5m long by 0.5m wide was opened against the left-hand wall near the cave entrance and away from the crush of tourists (**40**). The discovery of more human remains was unexpected as was evidence for more cut marks, but both were found in abundance. The finds were widely reported and distorted as shocking evidence of cannibalism by ancient Britons. The truth behind the headlines was that the broken bones of at least four adults and one child were recovered along with tools and animal bones.

These newly found human remains were carefully studied by Jill Cook of the British Museum. Cook is one of a small number of archaeologists who have been developing microscopic analysis techniques for distinguishing between natural marks on bone and those which are deliberately made by humans. Stone tool cut marks need to be separated from marks made by trampling, gnawing by animals and by roots growing around bone. Trampling by animals and people can produce deceptively human-like marks especially if the bone is lying in a stony deposit. Sharp stones can cut and scratch bones in ways which mimic the slicing of a flint knife. In such cases the position and patterning of the cut marks is vital in distinguishing between random and deliberate cuts. Studying cut marks also involves some practical experimentation such as throwing bones to hyaenas and observing the effects of their gnawing, or coercing friends and colleagues to walk across scatters of bone lying on different kinds of sediments. This is taphonomic research and good detective work.

Cook had already recognised irregular grooves on the human bones which were made by roots. The bones from the new excavations were different. Whereas the bones from 1928-9 had been varnished, the newly discovered remains were well preserved with clean surfaces and clear traces of knife cuts.

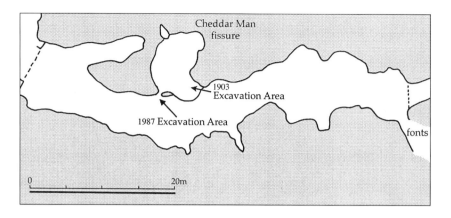

40   Plan of Gough's Cave showing the find spot of Cheddar Man (1903) and the location of the 1986-7 excavations (after Currant et al 1989).

Two of the adult specimens from 1986-7 show unambiguous cut marks made by a sharp stone edge on fresh bone. One skull cap or calvaria has cut marks along either side where chewing muscles attach and around the top of the head (**41**). The side cuts are evidence for the removal of the jaw from the skull and the marks around the crown were for the removal of the scalp. The cuts were made from front to back with the head probably facing up. There is more.

Andy Currant observes wryly that the edges of the skull had been deliberately to trimmed to make 'a fruit bowl' with the skull found lying upside down and filled with the bones of butchered red deer. For him, the fact that the humans bones were dismembered in exactly the same way as other animals speaks volumes. This was unadulterated cannibalism. One last clue which might have a bearing on the motive is the sign of a heavy blow suffered above the right eye. Was this ancestor of Cheddar Man simply clumsy or unlucky in warfare?

On the other adult specimen, a broken lower jaw, the cut marks are located where muscles connected the jaw to the skull. The cuts would, to quote Jill Cook, 'permit the detachment of the mandible from the skull and the removal of the tongue'. Similar treatment was meted out to a juvenile aged about twelve. Its partial upper jaw or maxilla shows cut marks to either side of the nose and below the cheekbones. The lower jaw has cut marks on the inside of the jaw giving access to the tongue.

There is more evidence of systematic treatment of the dead with cut marks found on other skeletal parts. Vertebrae are rare and of the four found two are from the neck and have cut marks where muscles of the back of the neck attach. It looks like the head was deliberately separated from the body after death. Limb bones are also rare as well as fragmented but some bear cut marks. The sample size is too small to find any particular pattern of dismemberment. Most of the other skeletal remains are ribs and among these there are some marks from cutting and *chopping*. Some of the ribs have breaks

41   *A 12,500-year-old skull from Gough's Cave with cutmarks above the ears and on the forehead. Is this evidence of cannibalism?*

where they join the vertebrae, as well as cut marks. It is not clear from these cut marks and patterns of breaks just what was intended.

The word cannibalism, as we have seen, does not explain the meaning behind the act. Was it part of a system of beliefs, evidence of conflict between groups or simply stone age barbarism of the type we are reluctant to admit? We do not like to think of our ancestors, and these are not all that distant, as having behaved badly to one another, but maybe that was how life was. We must remain open to that possibility.

The artist's touch

The human and animal bones found in 1986-7 were associated with a few stone tools and artefacts of mammoth ivory and reindeer antler. These tools, especially the ivory and antler, offer a clue to the context of the human bones. Mammoth ivory was a favourite material for Upper Palaeolithic people to carve and engrave and many of the finest examples of portable art are made on ivory. The ivory artefact found at Gough's Cave was part of the head of a spear or javelin which was probably hafted onto a wood or ivory shaft. The base of the ivory was bevelled to fit snugly into a shaft and cuts made around its base improved the hold of glue or perhaps tendons used to bind the pieces together. Other tiny ivory fragments were found which had been decorated with groups or sets of delicate engraved marks. Clusters of marks are usually considered to be **notations** or record-keeping systems (**42**). They were used to record events, count objects or perhaps to track the seasons and predict important periods in the hunter-gatherer calendar such as the migration of

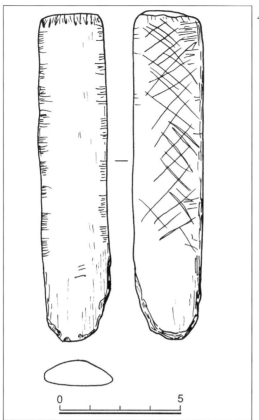

42 A shaped piece of animal rib bone from Gough's Cave with sets of lines or notations engraved along both edges (after Campbell 1977).

reindeer. Notation systems are further evidence of the well-developed use of symbols by modern humans.

Whatever their function, marked ivory and bone artefacts of this sort are features of the later Upper Palaeolithic of Europe. A classic antler artefact of the period was also found in the 1986-7 excavations. The *bâton de commandement* is an odd-shaped object. Made from the base of a reindeer antler with the tines cut away to create a natural handle and with a large hole drilled through the opposite end, the artefact has a slightly club-like appearance. Bâtons were once thought to have been held as symbols of status by the leaders of Upper Palaeolithic societies. This colourful interpretation has given way to a more functional view based on the study of wear patterns around and inside the hole. The Cheddar artefact has spiral grooves inside the hole (**43**). Similarly shaped artefacts were used by Native Americans to straighten the shafts of arrows and spears. Bâtons might also have been used to soften strips of leather or tendons. Whatever their particular function they were certainly well used items. Two very similar bâtons were found at Gough's Cave in Parry's 1928-9 excavations, bringing the total for the site to three. No other site in Britain can compare.

A final noteworthy object found in the recent excavations was an amber chunk. A larger piece was found in 1950 during excavations nearby and

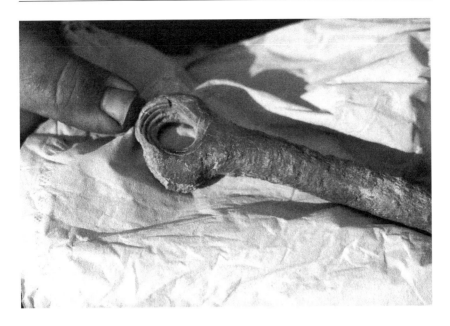

43   *The antler bâton found in the 1986-7 excavations at Gough's Cave with its
      spiral groove engraved along the rim of the hole.*

together they are interesting first, because amber is not local and secondly it
is not an obviously useful material. Today, amber is found on the east coast of
England where the North Sea currents bring it ashore from deposits along
the southern Baltic. Twelve thousand years ago world sea levels were still low
and most of the North Sea and Baltic were dry land. So where did the
Gough's Cave amber come from? One possibility is through long-distance
trade networks operating across northern Europe. Earlier in the Upper
Palaeolithic, fossil shells from eastern England found their way into caves in
Belgium. Perhaps amber moved along similar networks which started in the
Baltic region. Alternatively, a local source of amber was known to the
inhabitants of Gough's Cave, a source perhaps in glacial gravels now no
longer accessible. Or maybe it was brought directly to the cave by people who
had travelled from what is now the Baltic in the course of their seasonal
movements.

The question of source aside, amber is an unusual material to collect. It
lacks the glass-like properties of flint to make it flake in a predictable way, and
amber is too soft to be useful as a tool. The presence of amber at Gough's Cave
tells us that these people had things on their minds other than just scratching
a living. Perhaps the honey brown to reddish colour appealed to the occupants
of Cheddar, like the red of haematite used in the Paviland Cave burial. Or
could they have discovered, as the ancient Greeks had, that amber generates
static electricity when rubbed against fur, a unusual property in any age.

The fact that these various ivory, antler and amber artefacts were found
with the human bones makes the deposit more than just a dumping ground

of butchered bones and worn out tools. Analysis of the sediments and of surfaces of the bones shows that the deposits excavated in 1986-7 accumulated in a low energy environment, in other words they did not wash into cave, they belong together. Some of the animal bones were articulated and fragments of human bone could be refitted — these are indicators of a relatively undisturbed deposit. The associations of artefacts, human and animal bones are not accidental, at least not as a result of natural forces.

We come back to the evidence for human butchery and dismemberment and even cannibalism. Was it ritual or a result of warring between rival groups? Perhaps we are seeing a rite of passage, a death ritual, which we are ill prepared emotionally and intellectually to recognise in the archaeological record. These acts are too foreign and too far from our own experiences to be intelligible as the behaviour of our ancestors. Burial with grave goods we understand but a practice which involves de-fleshing and decapitating individuals rings no bells for us.

Before leaving this review of the evidence, we should consider two more aspects of the archaeological record of Gough's Cave. First, the 7,000 stone artefacts. That quantity combined with the various ivory and antler artefacts found since the 1920s can be interpreted as evidence that the cave was a home base or camp site of hunter-gatherers and not just a temporary stopping point. The shelter of the gorge, a source of water and perhaps some firewood all add to the attraction of the site. Given what we know of hunter-gatherers today, they tend to gather at favourable places in the landscape at times of plenty during a yearly cycle of movements. These *aggregation* sites are places where various groups meet to exchange information about the environment, to exchange gifts, to socialise and to find marriage partners. Cheddar might have been such a place 12,000 years ago, attracting otherwise dispersed groups of hunter-gatherers from the surrounding area. Perhaps the ivory and bone notations were markers for planning such gatherings or keeping track of the seasons to plan when and where next to meet. With relatively large numbers of people attracted to the area it may have become an important ritual centre as well. Aggregation sites, as today in the Kalahari or historically among the Plains Indians of North America, are places where rituals important to the community take place. Burying the dead in a ritually powerful or sacred place might be part of the attraction of the Gorge.

Where are the artists?

Cave art is one of the hallmarks of the Upper Palaeolithic of France and Spain which leads us to the question of why there are no painted caves in Britain? Decorated bone is known from Gough's Cave and a rib bone with a finely incised horse's head was found at Creswell Crags, Derbyshire (**44**) as well as a strange image of a part human, part animal creature. These are all objects classified as portable art and they have parallels in southern, central and eastern Europe. But only southern France and northern Spain have significant numbers of painted caves, more than 300 together. Having said that, the nearest painted site to Britain is a mere 100 miles (160km) south of

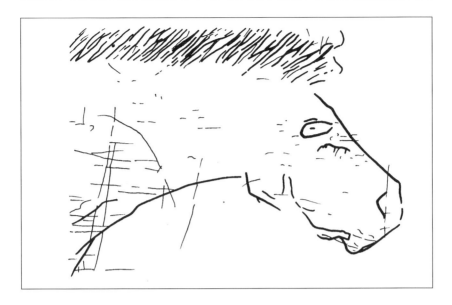

44   *A delicately engraved image of a horse's head from Robin Hood Cave at Creswell Crags, Derbyshire.*

Dover near Rouen in northern France. If so close then why has not a single undoubted site been found in Britain? The question is particularly relevant given a site like Gough's Cave which was clearly an important centre of occupation during the late glacial, a time of much painting further south.

Two possible answers come to mind: either they did not need to paint or the images simply have not survived the rigours of the British climate. Not needing to paint is frankly an unusual way to look at the problem. It suggests that painting fulfilled a need and the need did not exist outside the main areas of painting in France and Spain. What might the need have been? Clive Gamble argues that cave painting fostered a sense of group identity and this was especially important for coping with the pressures of a harsh glacial climate. Competition between groups of hunter-gatherers for the most favourable valleys — those with a mix of shelter, water, animals, plants and flint — would be most intense during periods of extreme cold such as during the Last Glacial Maximum. Painting is one means of reinforcing the traditions and identity of a group and perhaps for marking territorial boundaries. The need to maintain boundaries and a strong sense of belonging would relax as the climate improved and food resources became more widely distributed. This might explain why the long tradition of cave painting came to end with the close of the ice age when forests replaced tundra (see next chapter).

The absence of cave art in Britain could reflect a small human population coming and going from what must have been the very margins of inhabitable Europe. The numbers never added up to much and the pressures on resources were low which meant there was not the same need to keep investing time and energy in maintaining a territorial identity which was found further south. Painting simply was not necessary in this context. The few examples of portable art from Britain tell us that image making was part of the lives of these hunter-gatherers but that it was not confined to a particular cave or valley.

The alternative view is that some British caves were painted but thousands of years of weathering under glacial and postglacial conditions have destroyed the evidence. Robert Bednarik, an Australian rock art specialist, argues that the distribution of cave art across Europe today simply reflects different weathering conditions. Frost weathering in the caves of the Jura region of Germany, for example, might explain the lack of painted art in a region otherwise known for its portable art. In Britain, frost shattering may also have been a great destroyer even of the latest painted sites. A very cold period between 11,000 and 10,000 years ago saw the return of glaciers in Scotland and tundra like conditions elsewhere. Had Gough's Cave been painted it may have been subjected to frost weathering during this period. When water in limestone freezes it expands and the limestone simply shatters into angular fragments. Any painted and engraved surfaces would be destroyed. Even if areas of painting survived the cold they may have weathered away after the end of the ice age.

A simple experiment, in the courtyard of the Department of Archaeology at the University of Bristol, demonstrates just how quickly painted surfaces degrade under modern conditions. Using the kinds of pigments preferred by Upper Palaeolithic painters — haematite for red, charcoal for black and limonite for yellow — and mixing each with a bit of water to make a liquid, a group of undergraduates painted slabs of local limestone and sandstone. Images of animals, handprints and geometric designs were painted on both surfaces, each side with the same set of images. The students quickly realised just how skilled Upper Palaeolithic painters were. Making a decent likeness of a horse using shading and the other tricks of the time is not easy. The slabs once dry were set out around the courtyard leaning at a 45° angle against a wall. The upper side was exposed to wind, rain and sun and the under side was protected from rain but not frost. The next stage of the experiment involves recording the colours of the paints and taking photographs at monthly intervals over a period of twelve months.

Just four months into the experiment at the time of writing almost all traces of paint have been washed away from the exposed surfaces. That is not surprising. If Upper Palaeolithic people did paint on the outside of caves as well as near the mouths of caves then all traces would have long since vanished. What has been surprising is how rapidly the images on the undersides of the slabs have deteriorated. Some have completely disappeared (**45**). The red and the black faded and flaked off first with the yellow showing greater resilience but still weathering rapidly. In the four months since the slabs were painted the weather has been typical for the winter — the usual mix of wind and rain and a few days when temperatures fell below freezing but mostly within the seasonal average.

If conditions like this were typical during the last 10,000 years since the end of the Pleistocene and if caves were open to seasonal changes in atmospheric

84

45 *Paint weathering experiment in progress. A limestone slab was painted with charcoal (black), haematite (red) and limonite (yellow) and after 1 month (top) the images are still fresh but after only 3 months (bottom) they have almost disappeared.*

temperature then it seems unlikely that paintings would survive. The exception would be paintings placed deep in caves where the atmosphere and temperature remain constant throughout the year. Deep paintings have not been found in Britain and neither have engravings. Engraved images are an important part of cave art in France and Spain, especially the later art of the Magdalenian. If we look for a taphonomic explanation it might be a combination of frost shattering and water erosion or maybe some engravings remain to be found beneath the naturally deposited layers of calcium which blanket the walls of many caves.

Despite the absence of art on cave walls, there is some tantalising evidence of ritual activity deep in British caves. At Hoyle's Mouth, near Tenby in west Wales, flint artefacts similar to those from Gough's Cave were found 130ft (40m) from the entrance in complete darkness. Human bones came from the same chamber but, unfortunately, from a disturbed context. They may or may not be part of a ritual involving the offering of flint tools with the dead. A similarly enigmatic discovery was made at the cave complex of Creswell Crags in Derbyshire (see **35**). Here, deep into a long narrow chamber called

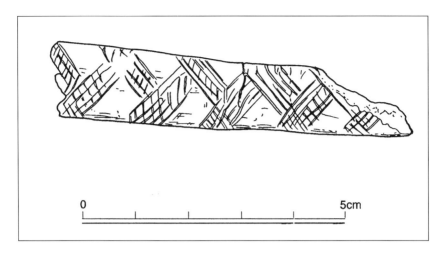

46   A piece of animal rib engraved with a zig-zag pattern from Pin Hole Cave at Creswell Crags, Derbyshire.

Pin Hole Cave, the fragmented remains of four people were found near two hearths, one in the centre of the chamber and the other hearth further to the back. Decorated bone artefacts were nearby, including an animal rib engraved with a zig-zag pattern of cross-hatches (**46**) and an engraved outline of a human being, the only image of its kind in Britain. These rare pieces of art seem to have been part of rituals involving the dark and the disposal of human remains.

On balance, the absence of both paintings and engravings deep in British caves supports Gamble's argument that art was not needed this far north. The social structure of these northern hunter-gatherers may have been different from those further south in France and Spain. Highly trained artists, for example, would not much of a role to play in the social world of Gough's Cave.

This is the kind of hypothesis that can be made once taphonomic biases are removed from the archaeological equation. The absence of painting and engraving at Cheddar might still be explainable on the grounds of a combination of natural forces working against their preservation. Another pigment experiment has just begun at Gough's Cave and at Wookey Hole to apply the methods learned in the courtyard in Bristol to actual sites in the Mendips. Spots of pigment have been placed on the entrances to both caves and will be monitored over a period of years. A detailed examination is planned for the ceiling of Gough's Cave in search of engravings. The results of both projects will not be known for some time, but in the interim we should work with a social explanation for the absence of art — it simply was not needed.

Getting a Result

Thursday 20 February 1997 Oxford is the worst place for traffic. I decide to go right around the northern ring-road to find the John Radcliffe Hospital. After almost circumnavigating the city of dreaming car factories and council estates I spy a signpost pointing to the hospital. The crew arrives just after me. We reconnoitre the exterior of the Molecular Medicine building. A couple of good shots of the name-plate and the not-bad modernist architecture. A bright sort of day with blue skies and scudding black and white clouds. I go in and ask for Bryan Sykes. He is a long time coming. I peruse the glossy literature for the Institute. Bryan arrives and we decide to do the DNA sequences first, re-creating the drilling of the jaw and the analysis of the samples in the laboratory followed by the results. 'Who,' I ask, 'is the descendant of Cheddar Man? Is it Vince Russett?' 'Don't know,' says Bryan. 'It's in the records.'

We film the drilling — or rather, a simulation of it. Bryan and his assistant go into a little sterile booth all togged up in sterile clothing with hats and masks and do the business with the bones. It looks good through the little reinforced window in the corridor. Modern medicine meets ancient man. We repeat some of the sequence in the main laboratory so we can get a jaw's eye view of the proceedings. Bryan talks to his assistant as we do this, his words muffled but audible behind his mask. 'It's a very nice jaw,' he says.

We follow Emilçe around the laboratory building up a picture of the processes involved in making gels from the samples of DNA taken at the school. More good science shots.

During a lull in the filming there is general conversation. John Podpadec, who actually filmed the taking of the samples at Cheddar, has not connected the two shoots and asks if we are looking at radiocarbon dating. At about the same time I reveal my general ignorance of the science of DNA. Bryan is critical; says it is everyone's duty to find out about DNA, it is so important. I agree, of course, but in this field I am working as a journalist, and sharing the ignorance of the viewing public, so if the explanations I obtain are clear to me then they will be clear to them.

Now for the results. We set up in a different room facing a light box to look at the gels; a computer screen; and a genetic map of ancient European DNA. I ask John to light Bryan with nice shadows. Bryan shows alarm. 'No. I'm not having that,' he insists. 'I know your game. Make me look like the mad scientist.' It turns out that Bryan once exchanged jobs for three months with a producer on Independent Television News, so he knows all the tricks. 'Nothing,' I reply, 'could be further from my mind.' John connects a monitor to the camera and shows Bryan the picture we are getting. It looks gorgeous, deep shadows, nice highlights. Warm. Relaxed. He accepts the picture and we get on with the film. First an interview piece where he outlines the work they do extracting and analysing ancient DNA. Bryan is very good at this, interesting to listen to, good to watch. Excellent material.

Emilçe joins us and the gel of Cheddar Man is displayed. Bryan points out a singular mutation at position 292. This is a distinct marker for CM's mitochondrial DNA, not present in control or comparison samples analysed at the same time. 'That's the feature we'll look for in the modern material,' he says. He puts up the Cheddar samples numbered 1 to 15 along the top. Here it comes. The result. 'Only one person with this feature at 292.' He traces the line of the DNA up to the top of the screen. 'Number fourteen,' he says, 'who is that?' Emilçe consults her list. 'Number fourteen; Adrian Targett.'

During the shooting of these sequences there is a to-ing and fro-ing of laboratory workers — Bryan's colleagues — in and out of the room. A woman in a white coat wanders up and looks at the gel of the modern samples from Cheddar. 'Oh, look at that.' She stabs her finger at a feature in the first or second column. Bryan shuts her up and shoos her away. 'What was that?' I ask. 'Nothing,' says Bryan. He may have said 'nothing to do with this,' but I can't be sure.

When we have finished shooting I am pleased with what we have got. We have got good visual and explanatory sequences. And we have a result. It is a good result because it is an adult and not one of the students. But it is not Vince, which is a bit of a disappointment. Driving back to Bristol to finish editing with Colette I stop to call one or two people with the news. We have got a result. It is magnificent. But its full significance has still to dawn on me.

Some days later I am driving up the Gorge past Gough's Cave. Who was Cheddar Man I wonder to myself? What was his way of life? Foraging through the woodland for fruits and nuts and edible vegetation; hunting for small and large mammals; collaborating with other hunters to drive animals over the cliffs or into traps or nets? What stories were told about these deeds? What legends of mighty hunters from the past? How were the spoils of the chase divided between the hunters, and their families, and the rest of the band or tribe? How did he dress? Spend his time? What was he called? And what did he call the place we now call Cheddar?

Most curious of all, how did he die? His burial has survived in a place that may have held more meaning in that time than a simple shelter from the elements. It is also likely that his death was not an ordinary one. The cave was clearly not where all the dead of the tribe were laid to rest. Over the thousands of years this place has been used by human beings it would by now be awash with bones — a veritable charnel-house. Its sparing use and the survival of so few intact skeletons suggests something more special.

I think of the face of Tollund Man, dug out of a Danish bog near Aarhus in 1952. Perfectly preserved in the peat, peaceful in repose — but in reality hanged by the neck until he was dead. Or strangled, on his knees, by someone standing beside him, then pushed face downwards into the bog, covered with a hurdle, and left there, perhaps to placate the gods or the spirit of the place, but in fact to be re-discovered by people nearly two thousand years into a future he could not begin to imagine. All is supposition. Ritual elements in burials suggest human sacrifice. Common criminals, who may also have been killed by a blow to the head, or strangled by an executioner, would not have been laid to rest so reverently.

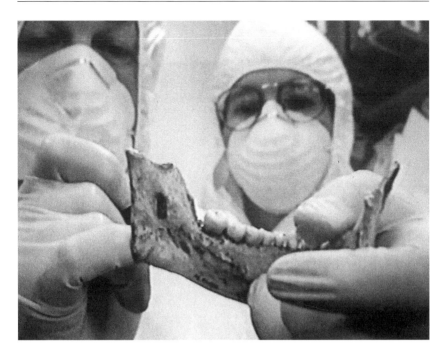

47   Bryan Sykes drilling the jaw.

On the other hand, Cheddar Man may have been a high status person, a warrior, a renowned hunter, a chieftain, a poet, or a priest. He might have been a storyteller, an oral historian of the tribe and its myths. He might even have been a visitor from Bristol — one of Bob Smart's limestone tourists —captured by hostile locals.

But if he had been sacrificed — or executed — we may imagine a scene where the abstraction of society was suddenly materialised, its values and beliefs and dominant purposes made manifest in the solemn rites of the ceremony. Official figures, dressed and decorated for the occasion, the assembled throng of the tribe, spoken words, prayers, incantations, exhortations — and at the centre of it all the appointed sacrificial victim, held fast not just by physical bonds but by the meta-physical power of the collectivity to which he or she belonged. Paralysed by fear, perhaps shitting him/herself at the last moment, but programmed by what we now call 'culture' into playing their allotted parts in the social drama without protest, or attempts to escape.

I reflect on our good fortune in establishing a DNA link over such a long period of time. I report the finding to Tom Archer at HTV. He is a journalist and sees what a big story it is. He wants me to talk to Richard Lister in the HTV press office, to make sure the story is properly aired. As I mull it all over it occurs to me that this might be an even more special discovery than I first thought. I call Bryan Sykes on the telephone. 'Is this the longest DNA genealogy ever established?' I ask. 'Yes it is,' he replies. I wonder why I have been left to work this out for myself. 'But not for long,' he continues; 'until August to be precise.' He will not be drawn on what he means. I assume there are older results somewhere due to be published in the scientific literature later in the year. But my immediate thought is that we have a world record on our hands. I think about trying the sell the story as an exclusive to a national newspaper — it might be worth several thousand pounds to Cheddar Man's descendant. On the other hand, an exclusive might not be taken up by other papers. Better to make it freely available.

Richard Lister says this is a world story. He will arrange for the Press Association to cover the story when we break it. The ideal time to release the story would be on the eve of the programme broadcast. On the other hand I want to film the announcement of the find at the school with Adrian and his students present to react to the news. This means publishing the story on the day we film the encounter and doing the broadcast later. The sooner the better. The story will leak out otherwise and we will lose control over the element of surprise.

I worry about Adrian and what we might be about to do to his life. I know virtually nothing about him, except his name and his job at the school, and the fact that he lives in a cottage at the bottom of the Gorge. But I know one thing about him that he does not yet know about himself. Something that may change his life. Put the teacher of history into the history he teaches. Will he want to be the descendant of Cheddar Man? Will the world's press descend on his doorstep? Will these archaeologists of disrepute dig for dirt in his past? Will the kids at the school call him 'The Caveman?' When you want publicity it is sometimes hard to get. When you don't want it, it can be even harder to get rid of.

Monday 24 February 1997 Dolly the Sheep hits the headlines. The first cloned mammal ever. Good news for us. Puts DNA on the agenda and into the mind of the media. The public view of science is always a double-edged thing — a sign of progress for the common good, and at the same time a threat to it — Mary Shelley's story of Frankenstein and the monster he created perfectly captures the dream and the nightmare. Flocks of pundits follow Dolly's story round the world bleating about the cloning of humans.

A couple of days before the declaration I let Mick Aston know the results of the tests and the identity of Cheddar Man's modern relation. Mick can't put a face to the name; he met so many people at the school, but his response reveals the mediaevalist he is at heart. 'Well, it's interesting,' he said, 'but in a way, so what?'

5 The big thaw

Ten thousand years ago the last ice age ended with a bang. Global temperatures increased, the ice sheets melted and the sea level rose. The distribution of plants and animals shifted dramatically and rapidly and the seasons changed. People living at Cheddar Gorge would have certainly noticed the winters becoming warmer, spring coming earlier and summers lasting longer. They noticed too that the familiar foods were becoming scarce, especially reindeer, giant deer and horse. Mammoths had already disappeared from the landscape some 2,000 years earlier. The short grasses and herbs of the tundra on which these herd animals fed were changing too, with birch, pine and juniper trees becoming ever more common. Decisions would have had to be made about the scheduling of the annual movement of camps. The elders of the group, with a lifetime's experience of hunting and gathering, would be called on to advise but they could not know that this was the end of an ice age. There would be no going back to the comfortable world of reindeer and tundra.

The end of the ice age was preceded by a 3,000-year roller-coaster ride of climate change. The people who lived and died at Gough's Cave 12,000 years ago experienced an interlude of warm conditions, an interstadial. The Late Glacial Interstadial as the period is known began about 13,000 years ago and ended 11,000 years ago with a return to glacial conditions. During this warm interval temperatures rose to near modern levels, the open tundra gave way to a mixed habitat with juniper and dwarf birch trees and later to full size birch. In this more wooded environment lived a mix of species for which there is no parallel today. From the animal bones excavated at Gough's Cave in 1986-7, Andy Currant has reconstructed the local bestiary living in and around the Gorge. The line-up includes wild horse, red deer, brown bear, lynx, woolly mammoth, wolf, arctic fox, arctic hare, aurochs and Saiga antelope (**48**). The latter is unusual being more commonly found in continental Europe and Siberia. Reindeer, the staple of the Upper Palaeolithic diet, was absent with the exception of an antler baton which may have been brought to the cave. The change from tundra to a more wooded habitat may simply not have suited the tastes of reindeer, but they did return as conditions became colder about 11,000 years ago.

The warm Late Glacial Interstadial was not without its own interruptions. About 12,000 years ago the climate suddenly turned cooler but this change only lasted about 200 years. The fluctuating climate may have been too much for mammoths because from about 12,000 BP they died out in Britain and

48 *Some of the large mammals living near Cheddar Gorge 12,000 years ago included (from left to right, top to bottom) woolly mammoth, Sika deer, horse, bear, aurochs, reindeer, lion and wolf. (after Barton 1997)*

disappeared across the continent. They may never have recovered from the very cold conditions of the Last Glacial Maximum from 18,000 to 15,000 years ago which reduced their numbers. Mammoths, like elephants today, were probably slow to reproduce. If climate was a factor in keeping numbers low then their continued hunting by humans would have sealed their fate — extinction was inevitable.

Had mammoths survived long enough to witness the return of glacial conditions between 11,000-10,000 years ago they would have faced another challenge with the end of the ice age. The return to glacial conditions may have only taken 20 years, an instant in geological time and an event which deeply affected the lives of everyone living in northern Europe. Glaciers formed once again in the highlands of Scotland and north Wales, summer temperatures dropped below 10°C (<50°F) and winter temperatures were a brisk -15° to -20°C (-60 to -70°F). An open tundra vegetation returned along with reindeer. This period, called the Loch Lomond Stadial in Britain after the Scottish centre of glaciation, was not just cold but also dry. Britain was inhospitable once again to humans. The residents of Gough's Cave left, moving south to warmer climes, along with everyone else living in Britain. Reindeer roamed for a brief time in a world free of humans.

The roller-coaster ride came to end with a bump. Temperatures rose rapidly about 10,000 years ago reaching modern levels in as little as 50 years. The effects on the environment and on humans were dramatic. The open tundra was colonised first by birch woodland and later by a greater mix of woodland species. Species like birch, juniper and alder could cope with the bare soils left by the retreating permafrost. For the animals which thrived on the tundra the change was profound. Reindeer moved north with the retreating tundra and today are found only on the arctic fringes of Scandinavia and Russia (they are also found in northern Canada and Alaska and are there known as caribou or wapiti). The grassland-loving horse also retreated from the advancing forest, finding a refuge in central Asia. The arctic fox and arctic hare likewise shifted their ranges northwards. In place of the reindeer the elk became the large deer of the European forest, its antler providing a useful replacement for making tools. Elk, like its North American counterpart the moose, prefers to spend much of its time in water and is at home around lakes. Red deer and wild cattle or aurochs survived the change and adapted well to the emerging forests of northern Europe. So too did the brown bear which had been a regular user of the caves of the Mendips, along with humans.

The bow and arrow

For hunters accustomed to preying on herds of reindeer and horse, the loss of the tundra forced some fundamental rethinking about how to make a living. A partial solution already existed in the technology of the Late Glacial. The bow and arrow was known and used for reindeer hunting by 12,000-10,000 years ago in what is now northern Germany. At the site of Stellmoor, more than 100 wooden arrows were found preserved in old lake sediments. Some still had their arrowheads, but they do not look like the nicely symmetrical artefacts of later times. These were slivers or blades of flint blunted along one edge to make a sharp point which was inserted into slots cut into the arrow shafts and glued. The pointed blades are called **microliths,** they are small and make lightweight tips for arrows (**49**).

Microliths can be flaked into geometric shapes such as triangles or crescents. Archaeologists use these shapes to recognise assemblages of tools of different ages and from different regions of Europe. Microliths are the artefacts most easily recognisable as tools of the **Mesolithic** period. The Mesolithic represents the people of the newly forested Europe of 10,000 years ago, who lived as hunters and gatherers until the arrival of farming and herding between 7,000 and 5,000 years ago. Microlithic technology and the bow and arrow appeared before the end of the ice age during the turbulent climate changes between 12,000 and 10,000 BP

By the time of Cheddar Man bow and arrow technology was widespread across Europe and had become an essential part of the daily lives of hunter-gatherers. There were no longer large herds of reindeer and horse to be stalked in the open where a hunter with a throwing spear could be successful. The animals of the forest, such as elk, red deer and wild boar do not travel in large herds or packs and have to be stalked individually. An arrow, unlike a

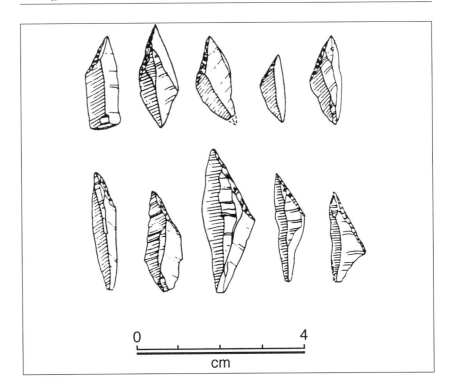

49   A typical range of microlithic artefacts made on small blades in the Mesolithic.
These would have been mounted, probably with resin, onto handles and shafts
to make a variety of composite tools.(after Mithen 1998)

spear, could be fired quickly and unobtrusively. It was an invention which came into its own with the end of the ice age. Examples of early Mesolithic bows have been found preserved in Danish peat bogs such as the Hölmgaard bow made of elm (**50**), which shows how large (1.6m) and powerful these weapons were.

The post-glacial world

The disappearance of herds of reindeer and horse had other dramatic effects on the lives of Adrian Targett's ancestors. Not only did a mainstay of the diet disappear, the seasonal cycle of moving camp to follow game also had to change. There was no longer a single focus in the lives of the hunters, the forest had different rhythms and new opportunities. The steadily rising sea level was drowning large areas of the northern European landscape and at the same time creating new coastlines and new sources of food. Fish, especially salmon, had been part of the lives of Upper Palaeolithic peoples living along major river valleys in Spain and France. Images of salmon and seals are sometimes seen in the cave art and on portable objects. Antler harpoons, which were distinctive tools of the late Upper Palaeolithic (**51**), took on new

50   *A reconstruction of the early Mesolithic Holmgaard bow made by Stuart Prior.*

importance as fish became an ever-growing part of the post-glacial diet. As well as fish, Mesolithic peoples became in time great consumers of the shellfish which flourished around the new coastlines of Europe.

Large areas of low-lying land in northern Europe disappeared beneath the waves of the North Sea and English Channel. Eighteen thousand years ago during the coldest period of the last glacial, sea level was 370ft (120m) below that of today. Within a thousand years — by 13,500 BP — the sea had risen an amazing 120ft (40m), nearly 13ft (4m) per century. The threat of sea level rise today as a result of global warming is a mere 20in (50cm) over the next 100 years. The change will be imperceptible compared with that experienced by our ancestors. As the great glaciers melted 10,000 years ago the ground beneath them responded, rising like so much foam rubber which had been squashed. Still, the sea level rose faster than the land around Britain. The Dogger Bank of the North Sea filled first by about 9,000 years ago and within a thousand years the straits of Dover were breached and Britain would soon be an island.

The large area of wetland known today as the Somerset Levels was also a creation of the rising sea level. A hundred feet (30m) beneath the Levels today lies a buried landscape of the Late Glacial. The rivers Axe and Yeo which today drain the Levels once flowed into a valley. Camp sites of hunter-

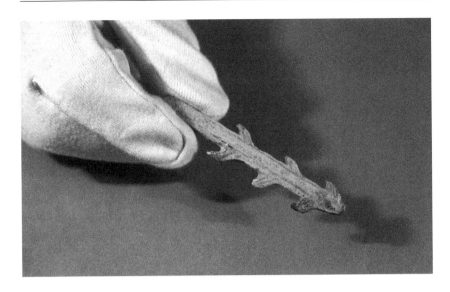

51   An antler harpoon with three barbs on each side found at Aveline's Hole (cast: Bristol City Museum).

gatherers who lived along the southern slopes of the Mendips are now also buried. As the Bristol Channel marched inland, the low lying valley of the Axe became a tidal estuary with silts and clays being deposited. Sand dunes formed along the coast creating a barrier which further blocked the free drainage of the streams and rivers. The town of Burnham on Sea, just down the coast from Cheddar, is built on one of these old dunes. Once the drainage of the water flowing down from the Mendips was impeded the estuary was colonised by reeds and the familiar peat beds of the Levels today began to form.

The hunter-gatherers of the Mendips would probably not have noticed the gradual encroachment of the Bristol Channel as it filled the Severn River basin over a period of three to four thousand years. The modern coastline of Britain was in place by 6000 BP. As the sea level rose the river valleys which had once carried glacial meltwaters were now being submerged. The result of this flooding was the creation of large estuaries and wetlands — rich habitats which supported migrating birds, fish, shellfish and attracted humans in search of food. The Severn Estuary today has the third highest tidal range in the world, and at low tide remnants of the old Mesolithic shoreline lay exposed. The first of more than 100 human footprints was discovered in 1986 on tidal mudflats near Newport, South Wales (**52**). Excavations since have shown the prints were made about 7,000-6,000 years ago, at the time the sea level reached its peak. Analysis of the prints paints a scene of family seaside outings with adults and children walking barefoot across the mudflats, probably from summer camps nearby. Their feet ranged in size from those of small children to that of an adult size 12 (British). Most trod carefully across the treacherous tidal ooze except for a child who managed to run. To

52 *Late Mesolithic human footprints preserved on the shore of the Severn estuary near Newport, Wales (photo: Stephen Aldhouse-Green).*

complete the day-trip to the seaside image, an antler tool for digging in soft sediment was found nearby in 1992 and proved to be the same age as the footprints.

The mudflats also preserve the tracks of other visitors to the shore including deer, aurochs and wading birds.

Historically, the Severn estuary and its tributary rivers have been famed fishing grounds for salmon and eel. Long tapering woven fish traps made of willow called **putcheons** (**53**) were and are still used along the estuary, with stainless steel now the preferred material. They are designed to take advantage of the tides, trapping the fish as the sea level drops. Putcheons bear a striking resemblance to 6,000-year-old Mesolithic fish traps found preserved in Danish peat bogs. The similarity in shape, size and material could be more than just coincidence; the putcheon may have a deep antiquity as a tried and tested design passed from generations of Mesolithic fishermen — and women — to the present. Coastal areas like the Severn estuary offer a potentially wide range of seasonal foods — plant, animal and marine — but to make the most of this abundance requires new technologies and strategies. Both were developed by later Mesolithic communities in northern Europe. The shallow waters and peat bogs of Denmark and Sweden provide well preserved evidence of permanent coastal settlements which thrived on a mix of resources. If such communities existed in Britain, their sites are probably now under water, but other clues survive.

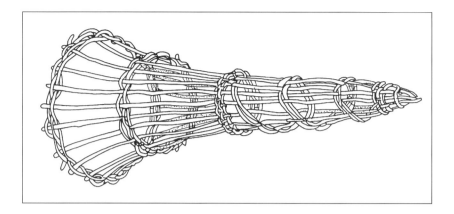

53   A wicker salmon trap or putcheon used by fishermen along the Severn estuary.

Refuse heaps of shell, or **middens**, have been found in western Scotland and in south-west England dating from the later part of the Mesolithic, after 8,000 years ago. A mix of shellfish such as oysters, limpets, scallops and winkles combined with deer meat may have been the basis of the permanent occupation of the western isles of Scotland. On the Isle of Portland, Dorset, the site of Culver Well (**54**) has revealed something like a settled village of people living in huts built on top of a large area covered by limestone slabs with cooking areas to one side. The local seafood was probably so abundant that people could live at the site for long periods of time, perhaps year round. Here they made stout pick-like tools for quarrying the local chert found in seams in the limestone. Portland chert was a valued trade item across the region and this community, thanks to the rich shellfish diet, had the time to become traders.

A healthy balance

The best-preserved coastal Mesolithic sites are found in southern Scandinavia. Among these, the now submerged site of Tybrind Vig in Denmark is among the most spectacular (**54**). Tools and food are preserved thanks to the water-logged conditions. They show a community based around fishing, gathering and hunting. Boats and paddles have been found along with fish hooks, spears, weirs and nets. Cod was the favourite fish. Its bones and scales are found in middens and in small clay pots, perhaps used to make fish soup (pots are a feature of the late Danish Mesolithic and have not been found in Britain). Vegetable foods also survive, especially hazelnut shells but also fruits, seeds and leaves. Deer and pig were part of what looks to be a well balanced diet. The quality of the diet is worth remembering when considering why these people and all other Mesolithic communities eventually adopted agriculture (see Chapter 6). Staying with Tybrind Vig for a moment longer, analysis of the chemical makeup of human bones from three burials confirms what the archaeological record shows, that these people ate a lot of seafood. A much

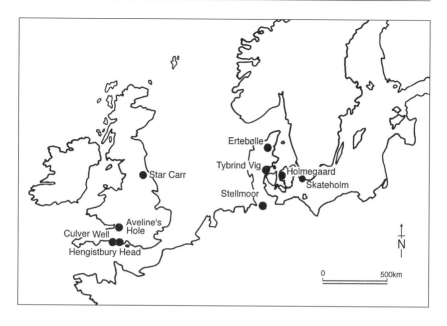

54   *Map of some important Late Glacial and Mesolithic sites in northern Europe.*

larger sample of human bones has been analysed from Mesolithic cemeteries in southern Sweden and Denmark with similar results.

Star Carr

Sites like Culver Well and Tybrind Vig are late in the Mesolithic and may not represent the lifestyle of Cheddar Man and his contemporaries. Many of the early sites, especially coastal camps, are submerged beneath the waters of the North Sea and the Bristol Channel. A famous exception is the inland site of Star Carr in the Vale of Pickering, North Yorkshire (**54**). Today the Vale is a flat bottomed and poorly drained valley covered in a blanket of peat much like the Somerset Levels. About 9,300 years ago when Star Carr was occupied the valley was a post-glacial landscape of lakes, ponds and reedy swamps. Star Carr is one of several Mesolithic lakeside camps in the area, the best preserved — thanks to the peat — and the most thoroughly studied — because of the exacting standards of recording and analysis set by the excavator Grahame Clark in 1954.

The remains of elk, aurochs, wild pig and red and roe deer have been studied to reconstruct what kind of camp Star Carr may have been and what time of year it was occupied. In the original report, the evidence of shed and unshed red deer antlers indicated a winter and spring occupation. Antlers were important in making barbed points for hunting and fishing and about 200 of these weapons were found at Star Carr (**55**). The collecting and storing of antler for making tools might just muddle the evidence for season of occupation and a more recent study of the animal teeth leads to a different

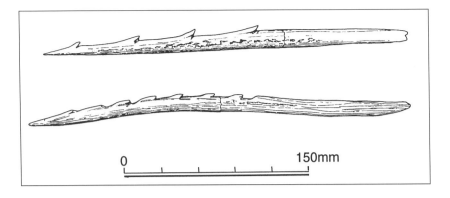

*55   Two examples of barbed points or harpoons made of antler from the early
Mesolithic site of Star Carr, Yorkshire.*

conclusion - that the site was used during the spring and summer months. Setting aside the question of when people lived beside the lake, the site itself gives a fascinating glimpse into camp life at the time of Cheddar Man.

As well as hunting large game, the people of Star Carr caught birds attracted to the lakeside including crane and white stork. No signs of fish were found, perhaps fish had not yet populated the post-glacial lakes, but analysis of the bone chemistry of a dog found at the site shows it ate marine foods, probably fish. Maybe the folk of Star Carr and their pet dog spent part of the year on the coast. They were certainly capable of fishing from small craft. A piece of wooden paddle hints at canoes being used on the lakes and ponds for transport and maybe for hunting elk and birds. Bundles of unused birch bark of different sizes were also found.

The birch was one of the first trees to colonise the postglacial landscape of northern Europe, and a useful tree it is. Its soft, flexible bark makes a strong container — birch bark boxes have been found in northern Russia and used to store flint. Birch bark is also water-resistant and was used at the late Mesolithic site of Eskmeals on the Cumbrian coast as a floor covering inside a dwelling. Being water resistant, the bark also makes a good covering for canoes like those made in the woodlands of North America. Birch trees also are a source of sticky resin which can be used as waterproofing and as a glue for fixing microliths to arrows. The most surprising use of birch trees is as a source of chewing gum. Wads of chewed birch resin complete with teeth marks are known across northern Europe. Chewing may have released antibacterial properties in the resin helping to keep teeth and gums disease free, not to mention freshening the breath after a heavy meal of elk stew. Elizabeth Aveling of Bradford University has studied the size of the tooth marks on this old gum and sees a pattern: most of the chewing was done by children and teenagers. But could they blow bubbles?

The birch and hazel forests of 9,000 years ago also provided a basic resource and one that it is easily taken for granted — firewood. Having unlimited firewood for cooking and heating would be a new experience for Adrian's ancestors. For much of the last ice age, trees in northern Europe would have grown in only a few sheltered valleys — like Cheddar Gorge, and not at all during especially cold phases. The scarcity of wood would make areas like Cheddar even more desirable and contribute to competition between groups of hunter-gatherers for use of the caves. With the end of the ice age and the spread of the forests this one source of tension would have disappeared with the reindeer and the horse.

The shells of hazel nuts, like those found at Star Carr, are a common discovery on many Mesolithic camp sites. The hazel tree offers nuts in the form of cobs and filberts and like most nuts they are rich in fat and a good source of energy. They also have the advantage that they can be dried or roasted over a fire and stored in their shells for months. Storing food, whether nuts or smoked fish and dried meat, was part of the Mesolithic strategy of smoothing out seasonal differences in the availability of foods. Vegetables were part of the diet but how large a part is hard to say because they rarely survive in the archaeological record. Looking at birch and hazel forests today, guesses can be made about what other foods would be available to early Mesolithic peoples, such as mushrooms, cow parsley, blackberries and perhaps even the roots of bracken if boiled. A lakeside environment like Star Carr would support reeds with edible roots. Analysis of the trace elements and chemical composition of human remains from inland sites like Gough's Cave would be very interesting indeed.

Before leaving Star Carr, one more artefact needs mentioning: a red deer antler frontlet. This is perhaps the most famous find because of Clark's interpretation of its ritual significance. The frontlet comprises the antlers and the top of the skull from which they grew. The skull portion has two holes on either side which allows the antlers to be worn like a hat. A reconstruction in the British Museum shows a bearded man wearing the antler headdress and a deer skin cloak. He could be simply a hunter disguised as a deer or more intriguingly a shaman taking the form of an animal to travel into the spirit world to intercede on behalf of humans. Compared with the Late Upper Palaeolithic with its rich tradition of painted caves and portable art, the early Mesolithic is strangely lacking in evidence for symbols and ritual. Why? The answer might lie in the upheaval of the end of the ice age.

Artists not needed

Twelve and a half thousand years ago when Gough's Cave was lived in by Adrian's ancestors, Upper Palaeolithic cave art was at its height. In France and Spain artists were producing beautifully observed images of horse and bison on cave walls and on portable tools of ivory and antler. The tradition of portable art with animal images had reached as far north as Creswell Crags in Derbyshire (see **44**), but, curiously, nothing similar has been found in the Mendip caves. From Gough's Cave there are decorated bone and antler artefacts with simple but intriguing clusters of deliberately placed marks (**42**, **56**). Some might not call this art but the marks are intentional and ordered in patterns which presumably meant something to the makers.

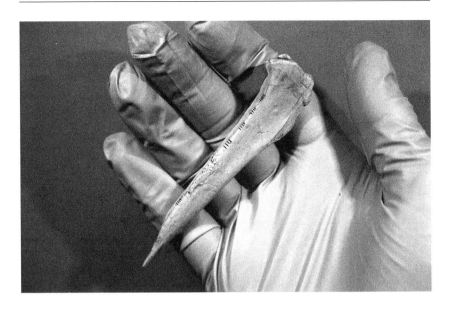

56   A pointed bone tool from Gough's Cave with engraved marks or notations (cast: Bristol City Museum).

Less obviously deliberate are engravings made on the top of a flint core found at the Late Glacial site of Hengistbury Head, near Bournemouth, Hampshire. Hengistbury reminds us that caves were not the only places people lived. Open-air camps were also the homes of Late Glacial hunters. The example of 'art' on flint from this site has parallels in France and Holland, but for most people it probably is a highly dubious piece. In its favour is the gradual shift toward less recognisable images of animals in the Late Glacial in favour of more geometric or abstract images. At Kendrick's Cave near Llandudno in north Wales, the upper jaw of a horse was engraved with sets of parallel zig-zag lines (**57**). The jaw has been radiocarbon dated to about 10,000 years ago — just at the very end of the Upper Palaeolithic. Unfortunately, the cave was excavated late last century before careful records were kept, but it seems to have been the site of a human burial with grave goods.

By 10,000 years ago cave painting as we know it from the late Upper Palaeolithic of France and Spain had come to an end. Walls and ceilings were no longer being painted or engraved. The only art which continues is that made on portable objects of stone, bone and antler and the images are very different from what went before. Is it a coincidence that cave painting ceased with the end of the last ice age? Is it also a coincidence that the art which continued — the portable art — was mostly geometric in design? These two changes are telling a story, but it is difficult to read after 10,000 years.

One explanation for the disappearance of life-like animal images is simply that the animals either became extinct or moved away. In other words, there were no more animals to paint. While it certainly is true that horse and bison

57 The upper jaw of a horse engraved with zig-zag lines from Kendrick's Cave, north Wales.

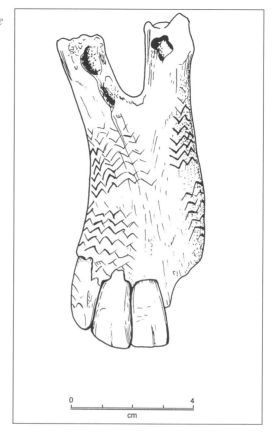

— the mainstay of cave art — disappeared from the landscape, other animals survived or new kinds of animals which could have been painted arrived with the forest. Red deer survived the great thaw to become the subject of much romantic nineteenth century painting such as Edwin Landseer's 'The Monarch of the Glen'. The small and delicately dappled roe deer moved north with the spreading forests and could equally have been a subject for painting, or the majestic elk, but neither was drawn. And why not the wild pig or the impressive aurochs? It seems clear that whatever needs cave painting fulfilled they no longer existed 10,000 years ago — the long tradition of art which began with the earliest modern humans in Europe was at an end.

If cave art had been a way of marking territories by hunter-gatherers, then the need for clear territories was now on the wane. Art can give people a sense of identity and of belonging to a place, just like a flag today or the colours of the local football team. In the lives of hunter-gatherers, a clear link to a particular valley or territory would be to their advantage if there was competition from other groups for land and resources. Under these conditions, art would not only be a rallying point for the group but would warn away others like a 'no trespassing' sign. Maybe the cold and dry phases of the Late Glacial were times of stress when competition for sheltered, resource rich valleys was at its greatest. Maybe, too, art was used to link people with caves and territories. Such territorial markers would reduce the risk of clashes or disputes over land and make life more predictable in a harsh world.

If painted art was used this way, then the end of the ice age meant an end of art. The warming of the climate, the spread of forests, the creation of new coastal habitats all reduced competition for food, shelter and resources like firewood. The spread of forests into northern Europe changed the social dynamics of the Late Glacial world. Art in its old role was no longer needed and neither were the highly trained artists. Artists who had been schooled in mixing paint formulas, in the use of shading, textures and surfaces of cave walls to make animal images come alive in a flickering light were no longer important. Perhaps the painter's role as part-time priest or shaman was still valued but a shaman does not have to be an artist to deal with the spirit world. If artists had enjoyed a privileged status in their communities then the coming of the forest was an equaliser of ice age society.

These are speculations of course; we can never know what the art meant but the fact remains that the painting and engraving of images of animals did come to end with the ice age. A new form of geometric art emerged with its roots in the Late Glacial. The art of the world of Cheddar Man was simple to look at and make but probably complex in its meaning. This paradox is seen in examples of engraved bone from Denmark. The humans are stick figures (**58**) and the other images are zig-zags. Zig-zags are common in the art of 10,000-9,000 years ago and easy to make. Little skill is needed, but knowing what the signs mean and how and when they were to be used might still be the role of a specialist. Even though geometric images do not look like anything in particular, they still have to be interpreted and explained. The person or group who knows what the images mean would have an importance and status as a result of their knowledge. Alternatively, the art and its meaning could be public knowledge and there would be no grounds for a specialist to interpret the signs.

Death in the Mesolithic

The question of who made and understood the art is a question about the organisation of the social world in which Cheddar Man lived. The most revealing evidence in many societies about the status of people in their lives comes with their treatment at death. Archaeologists rely heavily on burials and the objects placed with the dead for clues to the person's rank or status in life. It is a far from foolproof equation, but if a clear pattern emerges of a few burials having more things in them than is usual, or more valuable objects brought from long distances, then this could be a society with social ranking. Especially revealing are burials of infants and children with luxury items because children would not have had the time to achieve a status for themselves in their brief lives. They would not have had the chance to be recognised for their achievements as craftspeople, hunters, story tellers or whatever activities were valued. Rich offerings with children are a sign that they *inherited* their status from their family.

58　*A Mesolithic engraving on antler from Denmark showing a stylised human figure surrounded by geometric images.*

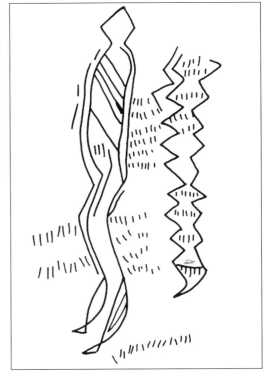

The man buried at Paviland Cave 26,000 years ago was buried with 24 mammoth ivory wands, two ivory bracelets, sea shell beads and lots of red ochre. He seems to have been someone special to have received such elaborate treatment. Ivory is not common in Upper Palaeolithic burials which makes the discovery of the bodies of two young boys from the 25,000-year-old open-air site of Sunghir, near Moscow, so fascinating. The children, laid head to head, were covered in thousands of ivory beads and had long ivory spears placed alongside as well as ivory daggers and the usual blanketing of red pigment. The boys were probably too young to have made much use of these weapons, and the carving of the beads and other artefacts involved an investment of time and energy by members of the community. The layout of the beads suggests that they were sewn onto the boys'clothing and that they wore hats. An adult male buried nearby received the same elaborate treatment. Were they related; what status did they hold to be worthy of such a spectacular send-off? The children were clearly unusual in death as they may have been in life.

What do burials tell us about the social world of the Mesolithic? Let's start with Cheddar Man. He was probably deliberately buried but unfortunately the accidental discovery of the body and the way it was removed means that evidence was lost forever. Certain details were noticed about the placement of the fingers and the skull near the knee which suggest a crouched burial. But what about grave goods? It was thought at the time that a reindeer antler bâton was part of the burial but that now seems unlikely, given what we now

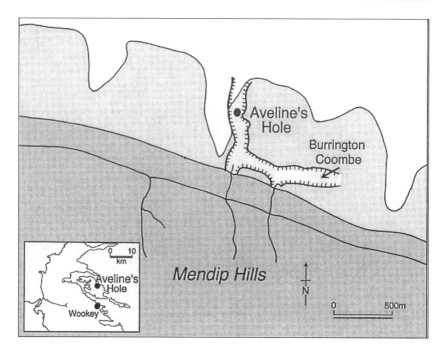

59   Burrington Combe and the location of Aveline's Hole (after Farrant 1996).

know about the age of bâtons. It was probably mixed in by accident, either when the grave was dug 9,000 years ago or when the bones were excavated in 1903. Piecing together which objects belonged with the body is now impossible. A clearer idea of how Adrian's ancestor treated their dead and the living can be found just across Mendip at the cave of Aveline's Hole.

Aveline's Hole - a Mesolithic cemetery?

On the Bristol side of Mendip, facing north, a small gorge called Burrington Combe cuts through the limestone (**59**). As the combe widens and opens to the modern traffic which uses this route as a shortcut across the top of Mendip to Wells and Cheddar, its cliffs expose several small caves. Among these is Aveline's Hole. The cave was discovered in 1797 by two hunters who chased a rabbit down a hole. After a bit of digging to widen the hole the two men entered a large chamber. The cave mouth through which they had dug was nearly sealed shut by a natural cement of calcium carbonate or **speleothem** and animal bones. The large entrance seen from the road today (**60**) is the result of several excavations begun early last century and in the 1860s by Boyd Dawkins and intermittently by the University of Bristol Spelaeological Society between 1914 and 1924.

The attraction of Aveline's Hole for several generations of archaeologists has been the presence of human burials. In 1829, an antiquarian published an account of various ancient sites in Somerset and described an extraordinary

60   The view from the entrance of Aveline's Hole.

scene inside Aveline's Hole. On the floor lay 50 bodies with the heads facing north. Reports of the time say the bones were encrusted with what we would recognise as speleothem. In later excavations, early Mesolithic artefacts and human bones were found to have come from a speleothem layer, which makes it likely that the 50 seen in 1829 were also early Mesolithic. Sadly and mysteriously, the skeletons had disappeared by the time the Boyd Dawkins began his excavations.

The Spelaeological Society in its excavations in 1914 found the remains of at least 11 more skulls and fragments of skeletons — Aveline's had been a cemetery. Judging by the type of flint blades found with the bones they were all probably buried about the time of Cheddar Man. Radiocarbon dating of bone has since confirmed the early Mesolithic age of the burials. Many more human bones were found between 1919-24, representing at least another 20 individuals. The bones were badly broken by falling blocks of limestone from the roof and by trampling, but some patterns could be seen.

In the jumble of human bones excavated by the Society — and the following information is taken from their Proceedings — a few individual burials could be recognised and a range of artefacts associated with them could be considered offerings or grave goods. Most unusual was the skull of a child that was broken into pieces, the pieces stacked and laid on top of an adult body in what may have been a ritual of some kind. In another area, the long leg and arm bones were parallel to the cave wall. Such an alignment might have been what the explorers of Aveline's Hole had seen two hundred years ago. The most common objects found with the bones were seashells which had been drilled to make beads. Perhaps bodies had been buried with shell necklaces or beads sewn to their clothing. A few teeth of pig and deer

107

were found that had been drilled or notched and these may have been toggles on clothing. Other more unusual grave goods included a cluster of seven fossil ammonites with one burial, a smooth red sandstone slab with another, a deer bone notched with two sets of six marks, and traces of red staining — possibly haematite — on two or three bodies.

Red pigment was a feature of the Paviland Cave burial in Wales and of Upper Palaeolithic burials in general, but apparently not part of early Mesolithic ritual. Perhaps the declining popularity of ochre use was part of a larger change in beliefs which took place at the end of the ice age, which included the abandonment of cave painting. Based on the evidence from Aveline's Hole, placing objects in burials does seem to have been a part of the treatment of the dead. What is not clear is the status of the individuals — were some people regarded more highly than others? The cluster of fossils found with the one body suggests that this person may have been someone special in the community, or was this simply an act of personal remembrance by family members? Aveline's Hole is just one site and a sample of one is too small to make any far-reaching conclusions. To make matters worse, much of the collection of bones and artefacts found by the Spelaeological Society was destroyed during the wartime bombing of Bristol City Museum in 1941. One spectacular find did survive, a barbed point or harpoon made of stag antler. The harpoon has two rows of three barbs (see **51**) unlike the single rowed barbs made at Star Carr (see **55**). The Aveline's Hole harpoon resembles Late Glacial barbed points found across northern Europe and may be older than the Mesolithic burials. Further excavation at the cave might clarify the age of the site and provide more clues about the local environment, but the chance to record an early Mesolithic cemetery is now gone. Archaeology is destructive, but even more so is modern warfare.

Large cemeteries are known from the later Mesolithic and a brief look at one, Skateholm in Sweden, could shed some light on the life of Adrian's ancestors. Skateholm was a coastal settlement with two cemeteries, the larger of which held 65 burials dating from about 6,000 years ago. Good preservation and careful excavation have given us an unparalleled glimpse of the treatment of the dead, both human and canine (**61**). Fifty seven burials belonged to humans with five of the graves holding two people making a total of sixty two humans. The remaining eight burials were reserved for dogs! Dogs were certainly part of early Mesolithic life with their bones found at Star Carr and Aveline's Hole. The Skateholm burials tell us that dogs were not just hunting companions but respected members of the community much like today's family pet or working dogs such as sheepdogs, terriers and retrievers. The dog, as an aside, was a companion for Mesolithic peoples across Europe and was the first animal to be domesticated by humans in the Old and New World. Its ancestor was the wolf.

The human burials show no particular pattern to the laying out of the body. Various poses or positions from sitting upright to lying flat out have been found. A few bodies were cremated to add to the range of options practised. A pattern does emerge in the positioning of the bodies by age and sex. The majority of female burials were in a flexed position with the legs tucked under

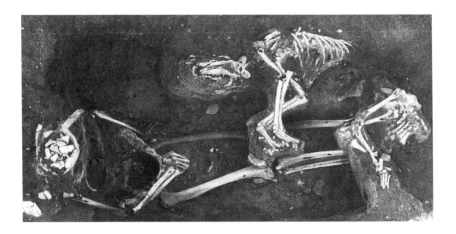

*61   A double burial of a woman in a seated position and a dog from the late
Mesolithic cemetery of Skateholm, southern Sweden (photo: Lars Larsson).*

the body, and the hands of the oldest women were placed in front of the face. Only six burials were of children and these were placed with adults, including a premature child found on the left hip of an adult woman of 35-40, perhaps its mother. The two bodies were covered in red ochre and the child lay on top of a cluster of thirty teeth of wild boar which had been drilled. Another burial of an adult with a child also showed special treatment of the young. The child was covered in red ochre and had drilled teeth — bear in this case — placed on its chest and four pieces of drilled amber under its body. Thinking back to Gough's Cave and the broken and cut-marked human bones, including two children of 12,000 years ago, amber was part of the assemblage.

In most hunter-gatherer (and farming) societies living without the benefits of modern medicine, the death rate for children is high, usually higher than the percentage (10%) seen at Skateholm. This could be a case of a high quality coastal diet enabling more children to grow to adults or perhaps children were usually buried elsewhere making those placed with the adults special cases. Is this evidence of status differences? Among adults, there is clear pattern in the distribution of grave goods with young females and older males having most of the offerings. Were they the most valued or respected members of this society? The grave goods are telling us something, at the very least this was not a simple group of egalitarian hunter-gatherers.

Finally, the burnt remains of an adult male with an arrowhead in his hip shows that life for at least this member of society came to a tragic end and is a reminder that competition between groups did not end with the ice age. If anything, the riches of the postglacial world may have led to population growth and increased stresses by the late Mesolithic. The evidence from cemeteries like Skateholm has a bearing on the issue of why these apparently successful hunter-gatherers adopted agriculture. The DNA extracted from Cheddar Man plays a big part in unravelling this mystery.

THE DECLARATION

Friday 7 March 1997 A cool grey morning in Chipping Sodbury; the kind of day not much loved by film-makers; overcast skies, quite a lot of light, but drab; the sort of day that seems to descend on gardening programmes. Driving shots were the order of *this* day. This film — another in the HTV series — is about the creation of mediaeval New Towns. Mick was to be seen arriving in the town from his previous location in an empty field not far from Cheddar as it happened — a place where the Pope's blessing had not been enough to ensure the survival of a planted market town. Here at Chipping Sodbury a similar enterprise had prospered. Mick drove up and down the main street. We shot him from the street and from inside the van and he spoke words to introduce us to this new site. Jill Ranford had brought a Pulnix lens with her — a very small, very wide-angle lens which she strapped onto the end of a pole and poked through the window of the van. The resulting shots are spectacular distortions. Mediaeval buildings curling through the edge of frame and Mick through the windscreen as though we were hovering twenty feet above the moving vehicle. Later in the day we planned to return to the empty field in Somerset to do some more linking pieces.

But before that we had a date with history at the school in Cheddar.

The mobile rang. Richard Lister from the HTV Press Office on the phone. 'There are people hanging around the school in Cheddar,' he says. 'How's that?" I ask. 'Well we had to brief the press and put them on their word not to blow the story before our embargo.' The Press Association man in Bristol is on holiday so Richard has asked South West News agency to handle the story. They have rung round a few trusted contacts. I know enough about journalists to know that you can only trust a lot of them to do only what is in their own interest. 'Richard!' I exclaim. 'Don't blow the story before I get there. Or I don't have a story.' 'Well, can you just ring the school, and tell them not to talk to any other reporters who may turn up?' I say I will do that. 'But on no account, I insist, 'must anyone breathe the name of Cheddar Man's relative.'

I return to the crew. Impious words escape my lips. The tension is getting to me. I ring the school. 'Yes, there is press interest. No, they won't say anything before we get there.' I report back to Richard. 'Don't ever do this to me again,' he says. The tension is getting to him.

We finish in Chipping Sodbury and drive to Cheddar. Park in the school car park. It is twelve thirty or so. I go into reception. While I am there someone rings the receptionist and says there is a film crew at one of the school entrances. I ask for Adrian Targett. A man passing through — it may have been the bursar — calls out, 'I expect it's him.' Does he know, or is he joking? I shrug in what I hope is a non-committal way. Will there be any element of surprise in what follows?

Bob Crampton, a reporter from HTV News, is there with a crew. They proceed to the chemistry laboratory to set up for the encounter. A reporter from South West News introduces himself, and his photographer — a young man with a monstrously long lens on his camera. Paparazzo meets the past. Adrian appears and some of the kids. Some of the ones in the original testing are not there. None of the adults from outside the school are present. I wonder if my failure to insist that particular students be there will have alerted Adrian to what lies in store. No sign of that. Everyone is more or less assembled. The HTV crew focus on Mick and Adrian and the students gather round in a semi-circle. Jill has put up some lights and is standing with our camera on a bench-top, ready to take in the whole scene including the other camera crew. Already we are spectators at our own spectacle.

> *Friday 7 March 1997* Have arranged for a science laboratory to be used for the filming and have contacted all the students who took the test and/or participated in the filming. Office 'phone at about 12.15 to say the T.V. team have arrived. Go to foyer: show Philip and the crew where the laboratory is: when the bell goes at 1.00pm get the students into the lab. As well as Philip's team, there is another T.V. crew here as well — HTV news wants to film the results too — so presumably there is a result! *Adrian Targett*

It is about 1.15pm. Cameras roll. I notice that Adrian is wearing a very smart orange shirt. Could be silk. Does he know? Has he dressed for the occasion? Mick drags out the moment like a conjuror with a concealed rabbit. We all know why we are all here. Do we remember the tests we took to see if anyone was related to Cheddar Man? Well the tests have come back, and there is one person present who is directly descended from the Man himself. And who is it? I think I sense a look of apprehension, maybe even horror is forming on Adrian's face as Mick turns to him. 'And that person is you — Adrian Targett.' I thought he was going to say, 'And this is your life' — but he didn't. Adrian gasped. 'Thank you very much,' he managed to say, 'thank you very much indeed.'

> To say I'm taken aback is an understatement. Murmur, 'Thank you very much. I'm overwhelmed' and realise why the microphone was put on me. The HTV news team take over and start interviewing me while a photographer snaps photos. Am told he is from South West News Agency, as is a reporter who wants to ask me questions as well. Am placed in the middle of a group of our students for photos to be taken. They look how I feel — shell shocked! The HTV news team interview some of them, they are a mixture of surprised and shy. Am asked how this discovery will affect my teaching. How do I know? Say it'll be a challenge to get Cheddar Man into 'The rise of the Nazis'.
> *Adrian Targett*

Bob Crampton is an experienced interviewer for HTV, a good interviewer,

62   The declaration.

but he seems at a bit of a loss — the moment perhaps just a bit too momentous to be captured in everyday words. They touch on the coincidence of Adrian teaching history. The students struggle to find things to say. The agency photographer takes pictures of Adrian with Mick. Adrian with the students. The headmaster wanders in. Mick shouts to him, making an overhead pointing gesture in parody of the National Lottery advert — 'It's him. It could be him.' In some ways the scene itself is an anti-climax. When we came to edit the sequence we had to work hard to make it work. Colette made pacy picture cuts and added lots of sound effects, general hubbub, camera clicks, a drum track, all to create a sense of frenzy. But it is not like that in reality. It is all very English. Very understated. It probably wasn't all that exciting when Neville Chamberlain stood in the doorway of his plane and waved his bit of paper from the meeting with Herr Hitler in Munich. He did it for the camera. It was a media event. This is a media event — only doubly so. A media event about a media event. Filming the filming. The history programme that made history.

After a while it is all over. The students have to go back to classes. Adrian is excused his scheduled teaching and the idea is to go up to the cave and do some more pictures and interviews there.

> Squeeze into someone's car and driven to gorge. Then go into caves to be filmed next to the replica of the skeleton. Bob Smart the Manager of the Museum kindly loans me a pair of Wellington boots and a pair of gloves, so I don't get too muddy.
> *Adrian Targett*

Jostle. Bustle. Down the cave to where another facsimile skeleton lies, all smiles and knees up, near the place where he was found. Happily this appears to have been on a photogenic ledge where all who pass can see him. We are standing by the railings that prevent enthusiastic viewers from falling onto the floor of the muddy grotto below. In the commotion I ask Adrian if the press agency has offered him any money for the story. 'I've signed a contract,' he said. 'Does it mention money?' 'I don't know — I don't think so.' I approach the young man from South West News. He confirms that in the few moments Adrian has been out of my sight he has got him to sign a contract. And that no money has been mentioned. 'Not good enough,' I say, 'lots of money in this story. What are you going to offer him?' 'I can't offer him anything. That's up to the partners.' The owners of the agency, he means. 'Phone them now.' We go outside into the gorge and he gets on his mobile. 'Fifty percent,' he announces. 'We'll give him fifty percent.' In the confusion, I can't remember if he amends the written contract Adrian has signed. That's the media business for you.

By this time Adrian is in the pit, on the ledge, crouching next to the copy of his kin, and smiling — like the celebrity he is about to become — at the camera. I watch with some trepidation, afraid of the tastelessness to which the press might invite Cheddar Man's new-found relation to stoop. I intend to step between them if anything goes too far. But Darren Fletcher, the agency photographer knows his business. He flashes away through the gloom with his long lens, thanks me politely, and departs to despatch his pictures by electronic means to Fleet Street — and then around the world.

Time is getting on. We troop out into the Gorge to film Adrian being interviewed by two reporters — one from the *Daily Mail* and one from the *Daily Express*. 'How old are you?' The old journalist's chestnut actually sounds quite appropriate to this story and in this setting. More than two hundred of Adrian's lifetimes would be needed to stretch back to the time of his ancestor. 'What's your wife's name?' 'Katie.' 'What does she think about this?' I give Adrian a mobile phone and get him to ring home.

> After being shown how to operate the thing I 'phone Katie. 'I'm in the gorge. I'm Cheddar Man!' Move away from reporter as I speak in case Katie isn't amused by this revelation. However, she says,' I know, I've got a reporter with me!'
> *Adrian Targett*

A look of wonderment spreads across Adrian's face. 'She says there's a reporter there,' he says. Fame has arrived — for fifteen minutes, or for longer. Who knows? By a string of accidents and happenstance, twists and turns of chance and choice, instant fame has come home to roost on one man's shoulder. Will he be all right?

Adrian has to go back to school. We arrange to meet him later outside the caves to do a final, reflective piece with Mick, and we go off to finish our work in the empty field not far from Cheddar. Our day ends with shots of Mick and Adrian emerging from Gough's Caves to balance the piece we

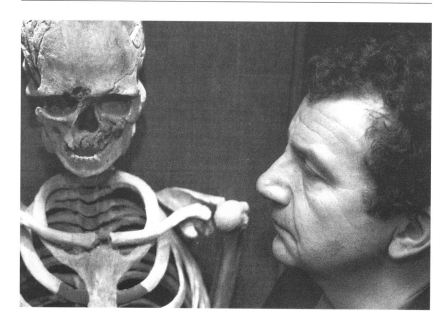

63   Adrian and relative (photo: Matthew Priestley).

filmed many weeks previously when Mick introduced this as one of the places in Britain where people had lived continuously for almost fifteen thousand years. We didn't know then what we certainly knew now.

> Finally Mick Aston and I are filmed talking outside the caves to provide an ending to the Cheddar programme: he finishes by saying, 'You'll have a rough few days ahead of you'. Mick and Philip think I should get an agent! I think they're kidding, but their expressions suggest not. *Adrian Targett*

We all repair to Mick's house for a glass of red wine to toast Adrian's new place in the history books.

> After school go with Katie and rest of 'Time Traveller' crew to Mick Aston's house to watch the local HTV news. It seems a big story — and it's a shock to see oneself on the television screen, though thankfully I was reasonably coherent.
>
> Get home to find LOTS of messages on the answering machine. As soon as I switch off machine to try and replay messages phone rings. Would I do an interview tomorrow? Agree. Put down phone; it rings again. Same procedure happens four times before I get to play other messages. They're all enquiries/offers for interviews. Note them all down.
>
> Go round to Mum and Dad's and tell them what's happened, They've seen the local news and can't quite believe it; tell them not to say anything if they're phoned, but to refer anyone to me.

114

> Don't want them to be exploited. Return home to find answering machine full AGAIN in only half an hour. Can see now why Richard Lister from HTV offered to pay for us to become ex-directory if it got too much! One message is from South West News with an offer of money from a tabloid newspaper if I'm willing to 'pose' as 'Cheddar Man'. I don't believe it!
> *Adrian Targett*

Later I watch the national News at Ten on ITV presented by Trevor MacDonald. I know that footage has been sent to them by HTV newsroom. The bulletin unwinds — nothing. Then Trevor says 'And finally...'. We are on the national news — and even though it is the 'funny' or 'strange but true' postscript, it is a sign that this is a story that will run and run.

> It's weird hearing Trevor MacDonald talking about me. Phone keeps ringing. Keep machine on. One of the messages is from the 'Today' programme on Radio 4. 'Would I like to be on tomorrow's programme?' It's been such a peculiar day: am whacked and don't call them back. At 11.30 pm I have to unplug the telephone from the socket so we can get some sleep. Perhaps I do need an agent!

> *Saturday 8 March 1997* Woken up by clock radio and the 'Today' programme. Dr. Bryan Sykes who tested the DNA samples is being interviewed about it; wish I'd called them back now. Listen a few minutes later to a review of the papers. From what I can gather I'm on a lot of the front pages. Go downstairs and get the paper off the mat. *The Telegraph* has a mention on the front page and half a page inside. It feels even weirder to be in the paper than it was being on the TV news.
> *Adrian Targett*

I rise. I do not shave. I do not eat. I drive down to the garage to buy all the morning papers. Bingo! The story is all over the front pages. Blimey! The story is all over the inside pages. It ranges — like the British national press itself — from the sublime to the ridiculous. An enormous picture, almost life-size, of Cheddar Man's skull stares out from the front page of *The Guardian*. Alongside, there is a smaller picture of Adrian, and a good story. Caveman jokes abound in the tabloids. Fred Flintstone is resurrected from ancient recesses in the sub-editorial mind. But there is a fine reflection in the *Daily Express* editorial on the marvels of modern science; a sense almost of religious awe.

> Get dressed and go to the newsagents. For the first time ever I buy ALL the papers - I'm on the front page of all of the broad sheets, and with a double page spread on nearly all the tabloids. There's even a comment in one or two of the editorials. Best

photo is I think the one in the *Express* with me and the students. The 'off the cuff' comment that Kate made to the reporter who interviewed her yesterday, as she was leaving, 'Now I know why he likes his steaks rare', is in every paper! The real joke is that how to cook meat is one of the few things we disagree on. Kate likes hers burnt to a cinder!

Phone keeps ringing. The tabloid paper has upped its offer to me to take off my clothes. NO! The calls are coming in from all over the world now. Do an interview over the phone to the London correspondent of the *Los Angeles Times*, Bill Montalban, and to a reporter from the *Philadelphia Enquirer*, Fawn Faure. After I've done the latter we phone Kate's cousin in Pennsylvania to tell her the story and to get her to buy an *Enquirer* for the archives. Natalie, friend and ex-colleague from school phones up. 'I was half asleep when the radio mentioned you in the papers. Was I dreaming?' Say 'No', and that I'm getting fed up with the phone calls. 'If you want to get away from it all, come over,' she says.

Keith Nuthall of the *Independent on Sunday* phones. He is doing an article about the science of DNA but wants to interview me as well, which he does over the phone. He also asks if he can have a photograph of me with Mum since this particular type of DNA comes down the female line. Have been reluctant to put Mum or Dad through the media circus, but agree to a photograph. Nuthall says an agency photographer will come. Mum and Dad come round after lunch. The agency photographer is from South West News — and he just happens to have a reporter with him who wants to interview Mum, the same one who interviewed Kate yesterday. Mum's mood is a mixture of the bemused and the sceptical and of course anti-science. She certainly gives the reporter a run for her money with comments like 'A skeleton in the cupboard's bad enough, but one in the family?' and 'It's weird — I don't believe it, and *my* mother certainly wouldn't have either'. Finally the photos are taken. As she leaves the reporter says, 'Your mother's certainly a bit of a joker isn't she?' I'm not sure who took most advantage of whom in that encounter!

Adrian Targett

I am thrilled. In a lifetime of agitation about this or that social issue I have done many press releases — have had stories in all the national papers, sometimes all at the same time. Some of those stories have drifted abroad — to the *Melbourne Herald*, the *New York Times* and once the *Papua New Guinea Times*. But none of them that I remember has ever been on the front page, and certainly not a front-page headline. This is a big story.

6 Down on the farm

More than 400 generations and 9,000 years separate Cheddar Man and Adrian Targett. The link between these two individuals is not just part of Adrian's family history, but it is also part of the history of modern Europeans. The Mesolithic is very much with us in the DNA of living Europeans. If that is true then what happened to the fishing, fowling, hunting and gathering lifestyle which seemed so successful? Adapting to a new way of making a living is not something to be taken lightly.

Changing jobs in the modern world is one thing — a supermarket is probably never far away — but to give up hunting and collecting for farming is a big decision. It affects where you live, how long you stay in one place, the tools you need and it will mean new rules to live by to keep the peace. Such a radical change might be attractive if farming looks to be the easier route to a quiet life or one that offers a more reliable and predictable source of food. Or, change might be forced on you by newcomers — invaders of your land. These are two very different options and until recently for most archaeologists the colonisation hypothesis has been the preferred explanation for the end of the Mesolithic. Colonisation seems to explain in a straightforward way the many differences in technology, settlement patterns and beliefs between Mesolithic peoples and early farmers. Adrian's blood ties with Cheddar Man have given us pause for thought.

The first farmers

Farming began in the Middle East 10,000 years ago. Archaeologists agree on that much, and most would also agree that the rapidly changing climate at the end of the ice age had a role to play. Just how large a role is a matter of debate. The end of the last ice age in the Middle East was not a simple matter of glaciers melting and tundra retreating, big game disappearing and the spreading of forests. The geography of the region is complex and being that much further south — Cheddar is 52°N in latitude and Jericho, an early agricultural site, is 32°N — the plant and animal communities of the Middle East were different from those of northern Europe. Temperatures were less extreme, forests survived in sheltered areas and edible wild grasses were widespread. The grasses included the wild ancestors of wheat (emmer and einkorn) and barley. On the grasslands lived a variety of grazing animals including sheep, goat, gazelles, onagers (wild ass) and aurochs (wild cattle). Red, roe and fallow deer lived on the fringes of patches of oak and pistachio

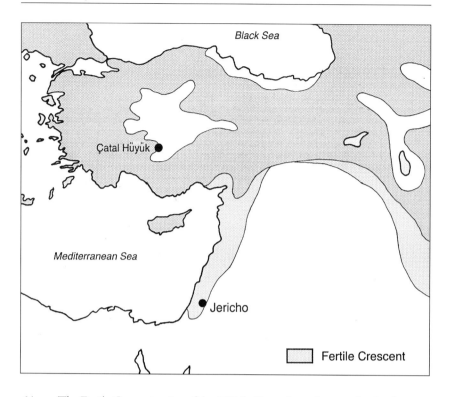

64   The Fertile Crescent region of the Middle East where plants and animals were first domesticated 10,000 years ago.

forests. Wild pigs rootled along the river valleys, fattening themselves on acorns and pistachios. Between 10,000-8,000 years ago almost all of these plants and animals (except deer, gazelle and onager) were brought under direct human control — they were domesticated. Explaining how and why this happened is one of the great challenges for archaeologists. The answers lie in the three millennia just before the end of the ice age.

The Fertile Crescent

The centre of domestication was the hilly region known as the Fertile Crescent. It takes its name from the rich mix of wild plant and animal foods found there and from its geography. The hills arc from the Negev desert in the west to the Zagros mountains of Iran in the east (**64**), spanning 1,300 miles (2,000km). Thirteen thousand years ago when the climate became warmer and wetter — just briefly — the wild grasses and forests expanded throughout the Fertile Crescent. Hunter-gatherers who had already been harvesting the grasses and hunting the game spread as well and their numbers grew. They used sickles made of curved wooden handles fitted with flint blades to harvest the thick stands of grasses. Grass seeds are a nuisance to gather and to separate from the stalks in small numbers but in large quantities they are more than worth the effort. The seeds were stored in mud brick bins and prepared for cooking by grinding and pounding.

This dependence on grasses combined with the technology for harvesting, grinding and storing grain set the stage for agriculture. The once mobile hunter-gatherers gradually settled down as they became ever more dependent on wild grasses as a basic source of nutrition. Storing food involves looking after your investment in time and energy and this means staying put. Grinding slabs are also heavy and bulky to carry around. The hunter-gatherer camps became small permanent villages based near sources of water and wild grain. More substantial houses with cobble and brick foundations were built. Along the western foot of the Crescent, from modern Damascus down through the Jordan Valley, the villages grew on the harvest of wild emmer and the hunting of gazelle. To the north, on the bend of the Crescent, wild einkorn was the grass of choice. Each area of the Fertile Crescent had its own preferred mix of plants and animals.

When the warm phase ended about 11,000 years ago — the same time that Britain became a polar desert — the now settled communities of the Fertile Crescent faced a stark choice. The option of returning to a nomadic hunter-gatherer existence had long since disappeared. There were too many mouths to feed thanks to the bountiful harvests of wild grain and the strategy of storing food. What to do? The answer was more of the same but better. The harsh cold and dry conditions of this period may have been the trigger which led some communities to experiment with the direct control of wheat and barley. The cold and dry spell only lasted about 200-300 years, but by the time warmer conditions returned domestication was underway. The rapid global warming of 10,000 years ago favoured the spread of grasses once again, but this time humans were involved.

Bigger and better

Domestication was not an invention pulled out of the blue. All hunter-gatherers are botanists and zoologists; they have to be to survive in a world of changing seasons. They know the habits of their plant and animal resources and the seasonal cycles of scarcity and abundance. As botanists, they understand the role of seeds in propagating plants and as zoologists, which animals are the most prolific and the most easily approached. The trivial equivalent today for the city dweller is being aware of the opening hours of the nearest supermarket during the Christmas and Easter holidays. A detailed knowledge of the natural world is something built up over generations and handed down through practical experience and through story telling.

Understanding nature's rhythms is the basis for the first simple steps toward domestication. It might begin with the innocent act of weeding or feeding which leads ultimately to the complete control of the life cycle of a plant or animal. Species which depend on humans for food, for protection and for reproduction are domesticated. Once this happens, people are in a position to *select* the features they find most appealing in a species and equally remove behaviours which are less desirable. In the case of wheat and barley the preference was for bigger and more grains per stalk, for stalks on which all the grains would ripen at the same time and for grains which would stay attached to the stalk when harvested. These are not the natural behaviours of wild wheat and barley, but they are the things humans wanted and chose. The domestication of goats, sheep, pigs and cattle was an extension of the principles of manipulation learned in the fields of the Fertile Crescent.

The domestication of grasses took place in the blink of evolution's eye, perhaps in just 300 years. Grasses are annuals and they grow quickly. They also will vary slightly in the wild thanks to random genetic mutations, with some individual stalks or seeds being larger and more flexible than others. These variations would have been noticed by those who harvested and threshed the grain. The first step on the road to domestication was to set aside these special seeds for planting and to eat the rest. In time, by artificial selection, a new domesticated species was created. When this first happened 10,000 years ago an evolutionary threshold was crossed. Human communities no longer relied on nature's bounty, they made their own. Rice, maize and wheat — all grasses — would be the foundations on which later civilisations arose in the Old and New Worlds. Billions today depend on this same small range of plants.

A price to pay

Farming can pay high dividends in the form of a reliable and predictable supply of food, but it comes at a price. Farmers are tied to the land; they may not have the freedom to pick up and move when the neighbours are difficult or the rains fail. Land itself becomes a source of wealth but also a potential source of poverty and conflict. Not all land is equally good for farming or grazing so early farming communities had to develop new rules for living to ensure fair access to land and its resources. A common solution around the world was to rely on the bonds of kinship. Groups of related families or clans would share the use of land, build communal structures for storage and defence. Clan meetings would also be the place for settling disputes. A council of wise old heads — the clan elders — would listen to the arguments and pass judgement. So long as the communities remained small, just a few hundred people at most, then kinship ties worked well to solve most problems. Nobody would be a stranger and everybody would be accountable to a clan for his or her behaviour.

Living in villages and towns does have a down side — disease. Cheddar Man probably lived in a social world of four or five other families, maybe numbering thirty people. Experienced campers know how quickly a site can become smelly and dirty without lavatories and rubbish bins. Hunter-gatherers simply pick up and move when conditions are ripe. Settled villagers have to cope with their own waste. Fatal diseases such as cholera are spread by unsanitary conditions and they spread quickly when people are living closely together. Domesticated animals such as cattle and pigs are another source of contagious diseases such as flu, smallpox and tuberculosis. The early farmers of the Middle East would have inherited some solutions to the

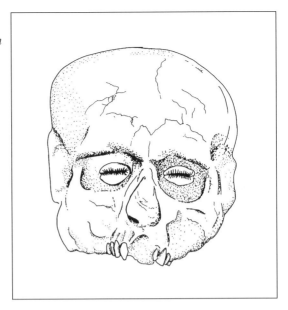

65 *A human skull covered in plaster with cowrie shell eyes from the early farming village of Jericho.*

physical and social problems of living in close quarters but living with sheep, goats, cattle and pigs was something new. After the initial exposure, deaths and illnesses, some natural immunity would develop to these diseases. These same animal-born diseases devastated the indigenous peoples of the New World who had no experience of Old World domesticates until the arrival of Europeans.

Farmers had — and still have — to cope with the many threats to their livelihood such as fickle weather and plagues of crop destroying pests. Frost, drought, floods and winds are some of the unpredictable natural hazards which make farming a risky business. Planning ahead is essential to ride out the worst that nature might inflict. Storing grain and preserving foods by drying, smoking and pickling are just a few strategies for long term survival. Perhaps the uncertainty of farming underlay the strong beliefs in the power of ancestors and the importance of ensuring animal and human fertility. These are recurring themes in the art and artefacts. At the early farming village of Jericho and elsewhere along the Fertile Crescent, the heads of the dead were removed and buried separately, sometimes with painted plaster imitation of skin and cowrie shells for eyes (**65**). Bodies were also buried beneath houses, as is the case at the remarkable 9,000-year-old town of Çatal Hüyük in central Turkey (see **64**).

Çatal Hüyük was the largest settlement of its day with anywhere between 2,000 and 10,000 inhabitants. The numbers were far greater than the few hundreds seen at contemporary villages. The complex of brick buildings being excavated at Çatal Hüyük by Ian Hodder, a Cambridge archaeologist, shows a community steeped in rituals inspired by farming. Common themes relate to fertility in nature and among humans, with wild bulls and female images — sometimes women giving birth to bulls — found in household shrines and larger communal shrines (**66**). Many layered wall paintings are a feature of the site, some with images of death linked to burials beneath the

121

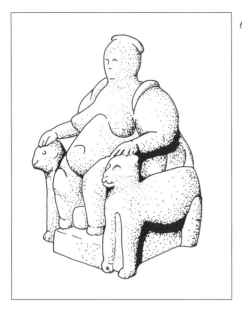

66   *Clay figurine of a seated woman from Çatal Hüyük, Turkey.*

floors of houses. The repainting of walls may be tied to the life cycle of the large families who lived together with two or more generations of parents, children and grandparents all under the same roof. This was a particularly wealthy community which owed its prosperity to trade. A natural glass-like material called obsidian was much in demand among farmers for making sickle blades and Çatal Hüyük controlled a particularly large source of obsidian in the mountains nearby. The farming communities of the Middle East and further afield were linked to each other by many small trade networks creating a web of contacts across the region. Through the web moved not just commodities but also ideas.

Spreading the news

By 8,000 years ago farming and herding had replaced hunting and gathering across the Fertile Crescent. Domesticated wheat, barley, sheep, goats, cattle and pigs were all part of a package of foods under human control which also included lentils, chickpeas and flax. The new economy and way of living proved to be hugely successful in other environments too, especially in Europe. Wheat, barley, sheep and goats appear first in south-east Europe about 9,000 years ago, then along the Mediterranean rim by 8,000 BP, and into central Europe 7,500 years ago. In central Europe, cattle and pigs were better suited to the cooler wetter environment and, after a brief pause, farming spreads northwards into Britain and Scandinavia by 6,000 BP. By archaeological standards, the changes that happened in those 2,000-3,000 years were quick — much like the earlier spread of the Upper Palaeolithic by *Homo sapiens*. The colonisation model has parallels with the Out of Africa theory. Both see the replacement of an indigenous population — in this case substitute Mesolithic hunter-gatherers for Neanderthals — by a group

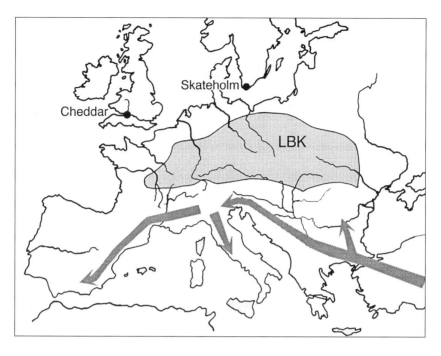

67   *The two main routes of entry of farming into Europe were along the Mediterranean rim (arrows) and up the fertile river valleys of central and northern Europe (LBK).*

equipped with a superior way of making a living. The speed of the replacement is powerful supporting evidence for both models.

Archaeologists record the spread of agriculture into Europe along two main routes: one up the river valleys of central Europe and from there into northern Europe, the other along the edges of the Mediterranean then up the Atlantic seaboard of western Europe (**67**). Each route has its distinctive styles of pottery, shapes of houses and mix of crops and animals. The farmers of central and western Europe settled along the rivers valleys with their fertile and easily ploughed soils. The glaciers of the last ice age had left behind a rich mantle of fine dust-like sediment called loess which attracted the earliest farming communities.

The cooler wetter climate and shorter growing season of central and northern Europe meant some changes had to be made to the Middle Eastern agricultural cycle. In reverse of the southern rhythm of planting in the autumn and harvesting in the spring, central European farmers planted in the spring and harvested in the autumn. It worked well. So too did the selection of cattle and pigs over sheep and goat. Cattle and pigs were better able to cope with the cold winters and forests. Winter feeding with hay also solved the problem of snow covered winter pasture. Cattle were not just good sources of meat, they could pull a plough, fertilise fields with their manure and their milk could be turned into storable foods like butter and cheese. This clever

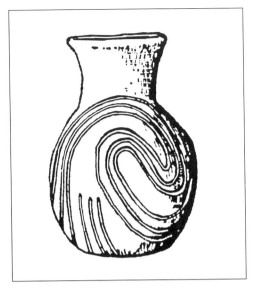

68   A Linienbandkeramik (LBK) pot with broad curving bands of decoration.

combination of adaptations to the central European environment fuelled the further spread of farming and herding. By 6,500 BP farmers were making clearings in the forests of northern France and eastwards across Poland and into northern Russia.

The northward spread of farming into Britain faced a minor obstacle in the form of the English Channel. Britain was by now isolated from the continent thanks to the rising post-glacial sea level. Any colonists would have had to arrive by boat. A lively picture emerges of leather boats stuffed with cattle, pigs, grain and families of farmers bobbing across the Channel to land on the uncharted shores of insular Mesolithic Britain. That is the vision of the colonisation model.

All the way with LBK, almost

The continental loess farmers decorated their pottery with bands of lines covering most of the body of the vessel (**68**). Archaeologists use the German term for this style: **Linienbandkeramik** or LBK for short. LBK communities also shared a particular type of wood working tool — the adze — and axes for clearing forests. Some Neolithic axes are made from flint, like Mesolithic axes, but also from hard igneous (volcanic) rocks which had to be quarried, then laboriously pecked and ground into shape (**69**). The smooth surfaces of these axes made them less likely to break and they gave a cleaner cut than their flaked flint cousins. As well as sharing ways of making artefacts, LBK communities also built their houses to very similar designs. The excavated foundations of these houses show them to be long and rectangular with large timber poles or trees used to support thatched roofs (**70**). The walls were plastered with a mixture of mud and straw over a lattice framework of branches. This *wattle* and *daub* construction was used for thousands of years afterwards well into Medieval times.

124

69   *A stone axe head of the kind made by early farmers in northern Europe for clearing forests. This artefact was found near Cheddar on the Mendip Hills.*

   The LBK longhouses are thought to have been the homes of single large families which may have included grandparents to make an extended family. Many of the floor plans show an open area near the middle of the house and this may have been where cattle and other animals were kept along with stored grain. LBK settlements are found as far north as Paris and east into Poland but the longhouses and banded pots, for some unknown reason, did not make their way to Britain or Scandinavia. Did the colonists leave their pots and house building skills behind on the shores of northern France and then suffer some collective amnesia on arrival in Britain? Unlikely. The radical alternative is that there were no immigrant farmers into north-western Europe, instead, indigenous communities of hunter-gatherers gradually adopted domesticated plants and animals into their existing ways of living. Through trade and other contacts they selectively absorbed elements of the farming life. That is the more modern and more complicated archaeological vision of how farming took hold in the north.

'Pick n' mix'

The archaeological record of southern Scandinavia during the late Mesolithic or Ertebølle period (6,600-5,200 BP) is rich in details of how people lived and treated their dead (as described in Chapter 5). The Ertebølle also overlaps in time with the arrival of LBK farmers in northern Europe. A closer look at this late Mesolithic community might reveal a clue about the interaction of

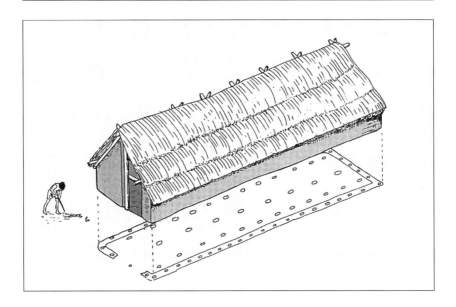

70   *A reconstruction of an LBK long house showing the floor plan as found by archaeologists.*

farmers and hunter-gatherers and help answer the question of how domestication found its way into Britain.

We know that Ertebølle peoples lived on a diet of foods from the sea and forests. The bone chemistry of the Skateholm and Tybrind Vig burials tells us so, as do the well preserved food remains from the living sites. In many ways these coastal villages were like the settled hunter-gatherers of Jericho who harvested wild grains and hunted gazelle. Both communities prospered, grew in size and stored foods. In the Middle East, when faced with a growing population and climate change the response was to domesticate. In southern Scandinavia, Ertebølle communities responded to their increasing numbers by intensifying their use of wild foods. Shellfish were collected in ever larger numbers, more effort was put into catching migrating waterfowl and people put to sea in large dugout canoes to fish and hunt seals, whales and porpoises. New and more complicated tools were made for fishing, fowling and hunting at sea.

Such intensification is probably a sign that late Mesolithic peoples, at least in southern Scandinavia, were under pressure. This may have been caused not just by having more mouths to feed but also by the combined effects of living in settled villages with the continued rise of sea level. The rising post-glacial sea not only drowned prime coastal sites — and many Ertebølle villages are now underwater — but also changed the salinity of the coastal waters, which could have made the shellfish beds less productive. These various stresses might explain the evidence for warfare seen in some cemeteries with burials, usually male, of people killed by arrows. There are even suggestions of cannibalism.

71   *A simple Ertebølle pot with*
      pointed base from
      Denmark.

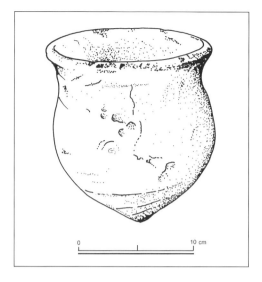

If this picture of a stressed late Mesolithic world is accurate — and it is controversial — then the arrival of wheat, cattle and pigs happened in the nick of time. Danish archaeologists have shown that farming communities in southern Scandinavia developed from the Mesolithic Ertebølle; there was no abrupt change in technology or in settlement patterns which might support the idea of an invasion by farmers. In the early phases of the Danish Neolithic, wheat and barley were grown on small forest clearings, domesticated animals were kept but people still hunted and fished as before. Only gradually did wheat, cattle and domesticated pigs become the mainstay of the diet.

Pottery was made by Ertebølle communities. Shaping and firing clay into a vessel is an idea that was probably borrowed from farmers further to the south. There are no other examples in the Mesolithic of this kind of technology before the arrival of farmers. Having said that, the Ertebølle bowls and dishes are plain and simple (**71**) and do not look like LBK ceramics, they are distinctly late Mesolithic. The borrowing of the idea of pottery and making it part of daily life could be just what happened with domestication. It was a foreign concept initially but the idea, and the plants and animals themselves, were adapted to an existing way of life. Existing trade links around the Baltic could have been the routes along which domesticates moved, from village to village, without the need for a migration of new people.

Might something similar have happened in Britain? It is not hard to imagine Adrian's ancestors gradually adopting farming when it became clear that growing a bit of wheat and keeping a few cows eased the burden of feeding a few more mouths or simply smoothed out seasonal variations in the supply of hazel nuts and oysters. Gradually, the investment in time and energy in maintaining fields, making hay for cattle and in storing foods would lead to changes in the lives of once mobile hunter-gatherers. A growing reliance on farmed foods would eventually disrupt the old seasonal rhythms like moving to the coast during the summer to fish, to the hills in the autumn to hunt and collect nuts and to the shelter of Cheddar Gorge during winter. New territories and new beliefs would emerge based on the needs of farming not hunting. In time, the lives of Cheddar Man's descendants changed out of all recognition.

This 'pick n' mix' approach to adopting agriculture puts the hunter-gatherers of the Mesolithic at the forefront of a major change in human history. It makes them active players in deciding their fate, not simply passive victims of an inevitable tidal wave of farmers. It also makes them more human, more accessible and a little bit more like us.

Language and genes

The big question arises again but now with added complexity: was agriculture carried across Europe by Middle Eastern colonists or was it an idea that spread among indigenous Mesolithic peoples along with a few seeds and animals? Or was it a bit of both? Pots and houses alone cannot give us the answer; archaeologists are adept at using the same evidence to argue both sides of the issue.

A new and complicating wrinkle has been added to the debate by Cambridge archaeologist Colin Renfrew. Renfrew believes that colonising farmers brought with them the languages spoken by modern Europeans. The Indo-European language family encompasses the many languages of Europe (and the Middle East, India and Pakistan) with a few interesting exceptions including the Basque language of the Spanish Pyrenees and the native languages of Finland, Estonia and Latvia. Renfrew sees Indo-European as the language family spoken by early farmers of 8,000 years ago who spread from Turkey (Anatolia) west into Europe. The successful farmers, and their languages, eventually swamped the smaller numbers of indigenous Mesolithic peoples, extinguishing them and their languages by 5,000 years ago. The debate then is not simply about the movement of peoples or ideas but also about loss of cultural identity.

Staunch support for the migration theory comes from another, non-archaeological quarter. The geneticist Luca Cavalli-Sforza of Stanford University, California, has spent more than forty years tracking the movements of prehistoric Europeans by looking at the genes of *living* Europeans. The approach is exciting because it bypasses the LBK pots and longhouses in favour of evidence that should be free of vested professional bias — genes. Genes do not lie, but unfortunately what they say is open to interpretation.

The genes which make each of us human and each of us unique are found in every cell of the body. From an evolutionary view, the most important genes are the ones passed from one generation to the next by fusion of sperm and egg. These genes are the true units of heredity. Every aspect of our being is influenced to some degree by this inheritance, from the shape of our earlobes to the size of our big toes. Genes have the task of making proteins, and proteins are the basis of cells, cells are the basis of organs, bones, blood

72 *A cross-section of a cell
showing the nucleus
and a mitochondrion
with its own strand of
DNA made of base
pairs of adenine (A)
with thymine (T) and
guanine (G) with
cytosine (C). (after
Suzuki and Knudtson
1990)*

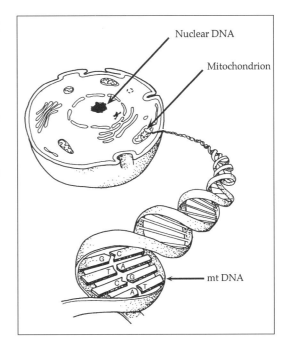

and the various tissues which make us recognisably human. Underlying this greatly oversimplified string of connections is the genetic code or sequence. The code is the recipe for making proteins and that recipe is written by DNA which consists of paired strands of deoxyribonucleic acid. The protein recipes all have only four basic ingredients called nucleic acids. They are known by their initial letters, A (adenine), C (cytosine), G (guanine) and T (thymine). These acids come together in base pairs — CG, GC, AT and TA — to form strings of DNA (**72**). In total there are 3,000 million pairs of bases in the typical human complement of genes or **genome** passed from one generation to the next. It is the ordering of this chemical alphabet and the lengths of the strings of bases which determine whether we are born a newt or an Isaac Newton.

Genes can be made of many thousands of base pairs — a long stretch of DNA — or of just a few hundred. We each carry about 100,000 genes in the **nucleus** of every cell arrayed in a regular order on bundles of protein called chromosomes. This 'nuclear DNA' is organised into 23 pairs of chromosomes in each nucleus, which includes one pair which determines whether we are male or female. When a cell divides so does its DNA and unless there is a rare mutation which changes the sequence of base pairs, the copy will be a faithful reproduction. The other source of variability comes from the mixing of DNA during sexual reproduction. The egg contains half of the mother's nuclear DNA and the sperm contributes half of the father's and together they make a complete set of 46 chromosomes. Each of us has a unique set of genes, thanks to the mix inherited from our parents. But there are similarities in the **patterns** of variation in closely related families, in local populations and even at the level of a species.

Genes can exist in more than one form and still do the same job of making blueprints for proteins. These workable variations are called **alleles** and they come into being mostly by mutation. Mutations are almost always eliminated because of their harmful side effects — they simply end up killing their hosts before they have children or leave their children impaired in some way. Some changes have little or no effect and these neutral mutations survive to be passed on to the next generation. Very occasionally, a mutation happens which is actually beneficial to the human host in a particular environment. In this case, the new gene or allele will be successful because the human host has been successful and the gene is passed on and spreads through a group becoming part of the inheritance of a population. Populations, in time, are characterised by large numbers of genes specific to that group.

Genetic differences begin to accumulate when populations become separated and no longer share nuclear DNA. The differences between the frequency of genes found in one population compared to another is called the 'genetic distance'. By comparing frequencies of alleles between populations it is possible to reconstruct their ancestry. Small groups of people with similar frequencies of genes are more closely related than those whose genes differ. Migration or movement of peoples is one way that differences accumulate. This is the thinking behind Cavalli-Sforza's research. He and his team studied the geographical distribution of 95 genes across Europe and the Middle East in search of patterns of variation which might reveal ancestral relationships. When their research began, the technology for studying genes directly did not exist. The analysis had to be based on indirect expressions of genes in the form of the distribution of the basic blood groups and other markers. Today, stretches of base pairs from individual genes can be cut and copied using PCR (see p53) for ease of comparison. These techniques of analysis have revolutionised the study of living and ancient DNA as seen in the case of the Neanderthal DNA.

In Cavalli-Sforza's research design, a prehistoric migration of farmers from the Middle East into Europe should be detectable in the genes of living Europeans. Not only would the gene frequencies differ between incoming farmers and indigenous hunters, but there would also be an echo of the movement of farmers in the modern geography of gene frequencies. As farmers spread westward their gene frequencies would become gradually less like those they left behind in the Middle East, being most different at the northernmost fringes of Europe. Their genetic distance would increase. The actual distribution of genes showed just that, a wave of advance of farming and farmers from the Middle East spreading west and north (**73**). Indigenous hunter-gatherers resisted the advance in the Basque region of the Pyrenees where the genes are least related to those of other Europeans. The survival of Basque as a language makes for a tidy correlation between Cavalli-Sforza's genetic map of Europe and Renfrew's map of the spread of Indo-European languages. Language and genes are a powerful combination in favour of the colonisation model. Here Cheddar Man and Adrian Targett enter the fray.

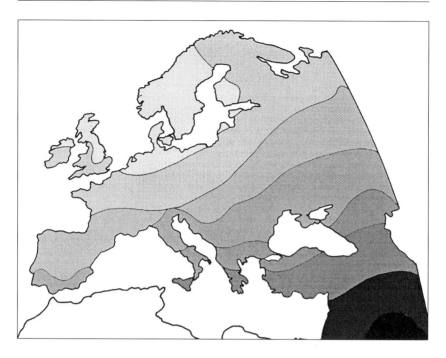

73   The 'wave of advance' model showing the spread of agriculture across Europe from the Middle East as based on genetic differences between living European populations (after Cavalli-Sforza et al 1994).

The Cheddar link

The discovery of Adrian's Mesolithic ancestry has transformed the issue of the origin of farming in Europe from a fusty academic debate to one of lively public interest. It is of interest not just to the Targett family or to the people of Cheddar and north Somerset. It involves the history of most modern Britons and in fact most Europeans. At its root is another kind of DNA, one which exists in every cell but not in the nucleus (see **72**). This is **mitochondrial** DNA (mtDNA) in its controversial role as genealogical tool, a role already seen in deciding the fate of Neanderthal.

Mitochondria are specialised units for producing the energy which powers individual cells. They have their own small complement of genes — about 16,500 — which makes them relatively easy to study compared to nuclear DNA. They have two other advantages for the geneticist interested in ancestry. This DNA is inherited from one generation to the next through the maternal line alone. The mother's mtDNA is inherited through the egg at conception but the father's mtDNA is in the tail of the sperm, and the tail drops off before conception. This feature of mtDNA makes it possible to trace the maternal ancestry of populations and individuals.

The most controversial feature of mtDNA is the rapid rate at which it accumulates mutations. Most mutations in nuclear DNA are detected and

131

repaired naturally but mtDNA lacks such repair mechanisms. One section of the mitochondrial genome called the **control region** does not code for any protein and is free to mutate rapidly. Parts of the control region mutate at ten times the rate of nuclear DNA, making them powerful tools for revealing differences between populations. (It was the control region of the Neanderthal mitochondrial DNA that the Munich team isolated and used in their ground-breaking analysis.) Mitochondrial DNA is also abundant with between 500-1000 copies per cell compared to only two copies of DNA in the cell nucleus. This happy quirk of fate means that mtDNA is much more likely to survive in the fossil record.

The rapid mutation rate of the control region makes mtDNA a potential **molecular clock** for dating evolutionary events. What is not certain is whether the rate of mutation is constant so some calibration is needed to set the molecular clock ticking. The rate of accumulation is measured against a known date, which can be an archaeological or an evolutionary event like the split between chimpanzees and humans, estimated to have happened 4-5 million years ago. The chimp/human divergence is the most commonly used benchmark in molecular dating. Pääbo and his team relied on this estimate combined with the mtDNA differences in the control region of living humans and chimps to calculate the age of our last shared ancestor with Neanderthals. The assumption of a constant rate of molecular change in this region of mtDNA is controversial. The rate of mutation is an estimate and may in reality have varied over time. Also, some mutations might be invisible having been lost or overwritten by later changes. There are statistical corrections that take these probabilities into account. But the best check on the rate of change is a well dated source of DNA, like the skeleton of Cheddar Man at 9,100 years old.

The search for ancient DNA in Cheddar Man resulted from earlier research carried out at Oxford University by a team of geneticists led by Bryan Sykes and Martin Richards. The Oxford team developed the theory that living Europeans are the direct descendants of the first *Homo sapiens* who entered the continent more than 40,000 years ago. Their theory emerged from a survey in 1991 of mtDNA from a sample of living Europeans. At the time they were looking at the Saxon migrations from Germany to Britain and part of the project involved comparing mtDNA extracted from Saxon skeletons with that of living Europeans. Included in the comparison was the mtDNA of modern Basque people. Recall that Cavalli-Sforza's research on the nuclear DNA of Basques showed them to be unrelated to other Europeans, a legacy of their Upper Palaeolithic ancestry protected by their mountain fortress of the Pyrenees. The mtDNA analysis could find no differences between Basques and other Europeans.

Either the Basques had been swamped by the genes of farmers after all or there was no mass migration and all Europeans were essentially the descendants of Mesolithic peoples.

74   *A network diagram of the 6 lineage groups identified in the mtDNA of living Europeans. Group 1 is the most common and the most ancient with its roots in the Upper Palaeolithic as represented by Cheddar Man and his ancestors at Gough's Cave. Group 2a reflects an immigrant population of farmers from the Middle East represented by LBK settlers (diagram courtesy of the NERC Ancient Biomolecules Initiative).*

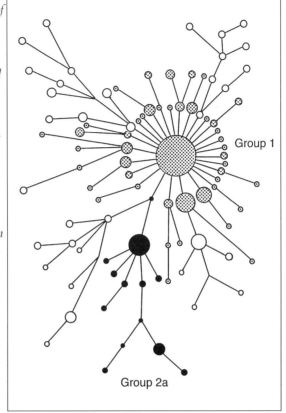

What's your lineage?

To test these unexpected results, the Oxford team sampled nearly 900 living individuals representing European and Middle Eastern populations. In theory, all members of an immigrant population will have more or less the same mtDNA base sequence or **haplotype**. After a few thousand years some mutations will happen naturally and become part of the genetic makeup of the population. Subtle differences will develop as the population grows, making for several haplotypes, each differing just slightly. These related haplotypes share a common ancestral lineage called **lineage groups**.

The tests revealed six lineage groups. The results are shown in figure **74** as a network of circles of differing sizes and lines linking them. This type of diagram is one way of presenting complex genetic data in a striking format that makes sense with a little explanation. Each circle represents a haplotype and the size of the circle reflects the frequency of that particular mtDNA sequence. The large circles are common haplotypes in a lineage group and the smaller outlying circles are mutations from the norm. The shorter the line linking two haplotypes the more closely they are related. Lineage groups are clusters of closely related haplotypes. In figure **74** the largest lineage group with the most common haplotypes is called Group 1. Radiating from this main lineage and connected by long lines are the remaining five groups, labelled Group 2a, 2b, 3, 4 and 5. Group 2a is the furthest removed from the others.

Comparing the number of mutations between groups, the Oxford team could date the various lineages based on an estimate of one mutation per 10,000 years. All the groups — *except 2a* — were old, having their roots in the Upper Palaeolithic, with the majority of haplotypes ranging in age between 24,000 and 50,000 years old. This meant that most Europeans — about 85% of the sample — could not be direct descendants of immigrant farmers from the Middle East. The remaining 15% belonged to Group 2a which was the youngest lineage ranging in age from 12,500 to 6,000 BP. This interval corresponds remarkably closely to that of the emergence of agriculture in the Fertile Crescent and its later spread into Europe. Group 2a haplotypes in fact resemble those found in Middle Eastern populations. This could be the faint signal of a small group of pioneering farmers who settled in a world of hunter-gatherers. The mtDNA results challenged directly the now traditional 'wave of advance' model. Some archaeological evidence was needed to put the two versions of the past to the test.

The next step was to compare the mtDNA of the six living lineage groups with ancient mtDNA extracted from human bone. Teeth were sampled from thirty skeletons representing LBK farmers in France and Germany and Upper Palaeolithic and Mesolithic hunter-gatherers in Britain (Gough's Cave). If the pioneer farmer theory was correct then the mtDNA from Cheddar Man should most closely match that of modern Europeans, and the mtDNA of LBK farmers that of the rare Middle Eastern haplotypes.

Jurassic Park is closed

The result is no longer a surprise but to prolong the suspense for a moment, mention should be made about the process of extracting ancient DNA from skeletons. It is tricky. Modern DNA is everywhere in our environment and the risk of contamination is great. The geneticist must wear protective clothing to keep his or her DNA from getting into the sample. A crumb of dandruff could do the trick and just breathing over the sample poses a risk. The air in the laboratory must also be filtered to keep out as much pollen and dust as possible. As an added precaution, the Oxford team copied their own mtDNA so it could be distinguished from that of the skeletons. Having taken all these steps, there is another hurdle to clear.

Time and temperature are the great destroyers of ancient DNA. When an organism dies, the proteins which make up the body begin to degrade rapidly and that includes DNA. Certain environments like cool caves are better bets for the survival of DNA which probably explains why Cheddar Man (**75**) and the original Neanderthal find retained fragments of mtDNA in their bones. For much of the rest of the world, such as the warmer tropics, the chances of finding intact DNA are poor and the older the bones the less likely DNA will survive. Fifty thousand years seems to be about the limit. Much of human evolution is out of bounds, not to mention the time of dinosaurs. The

75 *The extraction of ancient
DNA from a molar of
Cheddar Man involved
drilling under strictly
controlled laboratory conditions
to reduce the risk of
contamination by modern
DNA (photo: NERC
Ancient Biomolecules
Initiative).*

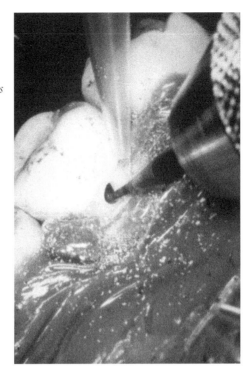

Jurassic Park fantasy of dinosaur DNA surviving trapped in amber for millions of years is just that, a fantasy. As part of the Ancient Biomolecules Initiative, a five-year project (1993-8) funded by the UK's Natural Environment Research Council, scientists at the Natural History Museum, London, looked at insects trapped in amber millions of years ago. Claims had been made early in the 1990s that DNA survived intact in amber and even in dinosaur bones. The London team could only find signs of modern contamination. How disappointing, but perhaps reassuring that modern humans will never come face to face with the likes of *Tyrannosaurus rex* or Stephen Spielberg's velociraptors.

Back to the results of the skeleton sampling. As of January 1998, the Oxford team had extracted fragments of mtDNA from four of the 30 skeletons. Two samples came from LBK farmers and two from Gough's Cave. The DNA of the LBK bodies was linked to the modern Middle Eastern lineage group; these were the pioneer farmers after all. Cheddar Man — as the world now knows — found a living descendant in Adrian Targett. A single mutation in the control region of the mtDNA separated Adrian and Cheddar Man. (The mutation rate of one change per 9,000 plus years closely matched Sykes' estimate.) This is not to say Adrian is the only descendant, he is probably one of millions who share the ancestral Upper Palaeolithic genetic inheritance. Adrian just happened to be the first to be found. Another was found in 1998, the chauffeur for the Marquis of Bath, and more will be identified in time.

The Late Glacial occupants of Gough's Cave who had so dramatically cut the jaws from their dead are also part of the story. Just as Cheddar Man is Adrian's ancestor, the people who lived and died at Cheddar Gorge 12,000 years ago were Cheddar Man's ancestors. Adrian's family tree has a few older branches.

Implications

A sample of four prehistoric skeletons is too small for us to be confident about their statistical significance. They are significant in other ways. They have fuelled a long simmering debate about the ancestry of modern Europeans. Arguments about styles of pottery and houses moving about the landscape have now been grounded in the lives of real human beings. Simple models of an inevitable spread of farmers at the expense of lowly indigenous hunters must be questioned. The spread of language and genes also looks too simplistic now. Archaeologists — and geneticists — can never take the past for granted and there is no certainty that today's explanation of events is the right one. It seems that the more we learn about the past the more complicated it is. Bryan Sykes and the Oxford team are currently recovering more mtDNA from their sample of 30 skeletons and submitting their samples to other labs for independent verification. Other geneticists will follow and the sample of prehistoric DNA will grow. As this chapter is being written, ancient human DNA is being extracted from the Mesolithic skeletons of Skateholm. Will it too fall into Sykes' Group 1 of ancestral European DNA?

In ten years' time the results of these pioneering analyses might themselves seem simplistic, but they have given archaeologists new information about the complex dynamics of human societies. In the 1980s, the steamroller model of farmers advancing across Europe came under close scrutiny by archaeologists, especially in Britain and Scandinavia. They openly questioned the old model of passive hunter-gatherers being replaced by farmers superior in numbers, technology and economy. It was time to consider just how hunters and farmers might have behaved when they met along the moving frontiers of prehistoric Europe. From the perspective of the hunter-gatherers, the presence of farmers living in settled communities changed the landscape not just physically but also politically, economically and socially. Farmers not only lived on the land which hunter-gatherers once used, they also changed the environment. They cleared forests to make room for crops and their cattle grazed where deer once fed. These physical changes meant that hunter-gatherers had to adopt — eventually — new strategies for making a living. Old foraging territories were altered as farmers settled in the landscape and their villages grew. Familiar trade routes and networks of alliances needed adjusting as did seasonal movements of camps. Gradually, over many generations, Mesolithic communities became inexorably tied into an increasingly agricultural and settled world. Joining the wider economy of herders and farmers was ultimately the only viable option. From the farmers' point of view, the Mesolithic peoples were not just competitors for resources but also possible partners in trade, labourers on their farms and sources of information about the world beyond the next patch of forest.

136

76 *A megalithic tomb from the 6,700- year-old cemetery of Carrowmore, Ireland.*

The interaction between foragers with farmers was complex, varying in kind and intensity from region to region. The transition was largely completed by 5,000 BP, but hunting, gathering and fishing — the mainstays of Mesolithic life — continued to be important to the emerging farming communities, as were their old beliefs in an afterlife. Along the Atlantic rim of western Europe, from Portugal to southern Scandinavia, the former heartland of coastal Mesolithic communities is littered with impressive stone tombs. These megalithic monuments to the dead were built in Brittany and Ireland (**76**) about 6,500 years ago and soon after appear in Britain, Iberia and across northern Europe. Many resemble in shape the timber longhouses of neighbouring LBK settlements, others are round like the huts of indigenous foragers. For some archaeologists, these tombs are a testament to the integration along the Atlantic frontier of old and the new ways of living and believing. Foragers and farmers alike took care in honouring their dead, but now the two traditions merged into a single monumental expression of reverence, one which left a permanent mark on the landscape.

This model of two communities interacting as near equals will change and be contested — that is the nature of archaeological inquiry. Gone for now is the simple equation of the spread of farming across Europe with waves of Middle Eastern immigrants. New discoveries, new ways of thinking and the recovery of ancient DNA have all created a new image of the past as a messy mixing of peoples and borrowing of ideas. Adrian Targett is the living proof.

Cheddar Man's Family Album

My mother and I.

My mother and I: Hilda Gibbings 1922-1997

My mother, Hilda Gibbings, was one of 13 children born to my grandparents, Elizabeth and James Gibbings. My mother had two brothers and ten sisters, and she was a half of one of the four sets of non-identical twins born to my grandmother. One of the last pair of twins died whilst an infant, but the other 12 children all grew to adulthood and ten of them are still alive today. Granny used to say she felt fortunate to have reared her family and only lost one child: 'I hadn't meant to have so many children, but I was glad to have had them, and to have been able to rear them all except one.'

I grew up in Bedminster on the edge of Totterdown in Bristol in the late 1950s and early 1960s. St Luke's Road consisted of two ranks of terraced houses. Until I was six we lived at number 108 on the Totterdown side. These were two-up, two-down houses dating from the late 1860s and early 1870s, with a lean-to kitchen, a backyard and a pocket handkerchief of a front garden with steps down to the pavement.

There are photographs taken of my mother and some of her sisters whilst at school, showing them in line as pairs of twins, oldest to youngest. Some of the girls are wearing boots. On pointing this out to one of my aunties, she replied , 'They were "Lord Mayor's Boots" — as a poor family we got them from the Lord Mayor's boot appeal. They had lots of studs in them to save the soles and when the boots were new we could "strike fire" with them, which was fun.'

As well as having free shoes, growing up as part of a large, poor family in a fairly small house led to domestic arrangements which today must be fairly unusual. 'As young children,' my mother said, 'we all slept sideways head to toe across one big bed so that we'd all fit in — just like sardines in a tin.'

Granny Gibbings, as a young woman.

Granny Gibbings 1890-1972

My grandmother, born Elizabeth Beaven in 1890, was in many ways Victorian in her attitudes and outlook. She told me how as a girl of about nine she stood at the bottom of 'The Incline' — the approach road to Temple Meads Station and had seen Queen Victoria in her carriage when she visited Bristol in 1899. I concluded from the way she described it that it had been an 'experience'. 'Everybody was cheering,' she said, 'and I managed to get to the front of the crowd. I could just see this tiny old woman all in black under a parasol, nodding her head to the cheers and the waves. It seemed funny to me that she was Queen of such a large Empire.'

Like most girls of her class and generation Granny had only a basic elementary education and what she received didn't really do justice to her intellect. She was an intelligent and astute woman. If I or my cousins moaned to her about school, she'd invariably say, 'I went to school up Redcliffe. We had to pay 2d. a week on Mondays in order to go. I used to tell our mother to be sure to keep back the 2d., "as I'm not staying home".'

Her daughter Faith remembers: 'Our mother used to say "Reading is Intelligence". She used to send us over to Bedminster Library and tell us to make full use of the facilities. As a result her children were able to get good jobs, such as in Wills or Mardons.'

Great Granny Thomas.

Great Granny Thomas 1867-1947

If my grandmother exhibited some Victorian characteristics, then her mother, my great-grandmother, was the full-blown Victorian matriarch, both in character and appearance. She had been born Sarah Ann Richards in 1867, at 91, Philip Street, Bedminster, the youngest child of Charles Richards, journeyman baker and Sarah Ann, formerly Lute. From 1917 until she died in 1947, my great-grandmother lived at 64 Whitehouse Lane, just around the corner from Philip Street. For some years after the demolition of these houses and the clearing of former industrial sites such as the tannery and Capper Pass smelting works, the area remained a neglected wasteland. Now there are small industrial units and businesses and the site of Granny Thomas's house in Whitehouse Lane is part of the City Farm. For a few years from 1913 to 1917 she lived at 2, Regent Road where she owned and ran a sweetshop from her front room. In later years this area saw the demolition of the houses and the building of Bedminster Library, the extension of Wills' factory — and subsequently the Asda supermarket.

Sarah Ann married twice: firstly in 1885 my great-grandfather William Beaven, who was a railway worker and died in his thirties, and by whom she had six children, including my grandmother. Secondly my great-grandmother married Edward Thomas, who worked for Bristol Corporation and by whom she had a further ten children. Of the six children of the first marriage, four survived to adulthood. A son, Charles Joseph Beaven died aged seven weeks and a daughter Jane Beaven died of TB at the age of sixteen. Of the ten children of the second marriage, a boy Arthur Thomas and the twins Violet and Ada died at six weeks. The eldest son Jack Thomas was killed at the Battle of Jutland in 1918. Another son George Thomas, who served in the Merchant Navy, died on a hospital ship, presumably of wounds, in 1918. Three other children William Beaven, Edward Thomas and Gilbert Thomas were also linked with the sea.

Sarah Anne Lute's birth certificate

William and Gilbert were both actively involved in the National Union of Seamen and it was partly as a consequence of this work that the last mentioned of the three, Gilbert, became Sheriff of Bristol in 1968.

Sarah Ann Lute b. 1837

Granny Thomas obviously took family matters seriously. Her family Bible records the births and names of all of her children and even the registration entry numbers when the births were registered. Little however was known about Granny Thomas herself. Her grandchildren cannot recollect her talking about her early life or family. I was keen to try and go back at least another generation if I could. I knew from the Bible when she was born so I applied to the Register office in Quakers Friars in Bristol, for a copy of her birth certificate. This came up with some of the answers, such as the names of her parents — Charles and Sarah Ann Richards, her date and place of birth (on 1 May 1867 at 91, Philip Street, Bedminster), her father's profession (journeyman baker) and her mother's maiden name (SUTE).

The last-mentioned name rather puzzled me since I had never heard of such a name. In the Bristol Reference Library consultation of the 1861 Census index reinforced this view. Then I decided to apply for the birth certificate of Sarah Ann's elder brother Jesse. The details on it were very similar except for two facts — Jesse was born at 89, Philip Street, next door from Sarah Ann's birthplace and the maiden name of his mother was LUTE. Presumably the Victorian copperplate Ls and Ss were easily confused.

Further research suggested that Granny Thomas's mother Sarah Ann Lute was born in the second half of 1837. This was very fortunate since the national registration of births, marriages and deaths only began earlier that year. I applied for the certificate and only a few days later it arrived in the post. Sarah Ann Lute was born on 28 August 1837 at Nelson's Gardens, Redcliff, Bristol, to Thomas and Sarah Lute.

One coincidence is that Sarah Ann's father, and her husband, Charles Richards were both bakers. The other is that Sarah Lute's maiden name was Howell, which is the same surname as my wife's mother's maiden name. Sarah Lute's mother was another Sarah — Sarah Howell, born 1807, died 1878. My wife's great great grandfather, Benjamin Howell was also born in Redcliff. Is there a connection therefore between our two families?

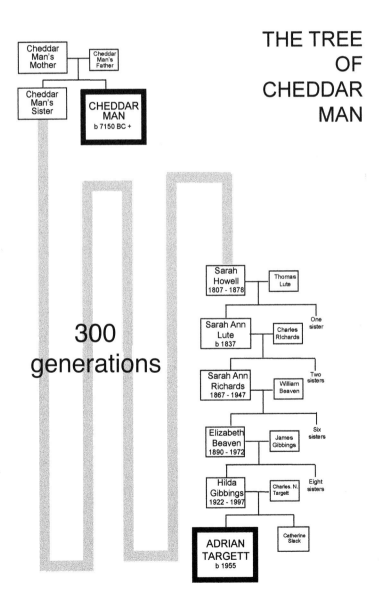

THE TREE OF CHEDDAR MAN

7 The legacy of bones

'All progress is based upon a universal innate desire on the part of every organism to live beyond its income.' Samuel Butler 1912 (novelist, painter, philosopher and scholar)

Adrian Targett and Cheddar Man are relatives — their genes tell us so — and Cheddar Gorge has been home to both of them at different times. Other than this, their lives have nothing obvious in common. That said, Cheddar Gorge has changed. Nine thousand years of weathering have made a slight difference to its appearance, but it is farming, mining and now tourism which will have altered the local landscape beyond recognition to the eyes of a hunter-gatherer. So even the Gorge is really not common ground between the two men. That leaves the ancestral bones as Adrian's link to the past and Cheddar Man's link to the future.

The recovery of ancient human DNA is a stunning achievement of modern science and a boon for constructing distant family trees. Genes can tell us where we have come from and how closely we are related to each other and to other human species. But they say almost nothing when we ask questions about how people lived, what they believed in and thought about. Until time machines are invented our only hope of answering these questions is to look to the archaeological record. The answers lie in the unglamorous world which we have been looking at of broken stone blades, fragments of pots, scatters of pigment and bits of animal bones.

Very rarely is the archaeologist treated to a site like Yorkshire's Star Carr which preserves the details of daily routines. What we see there enables us to piece together evidence for the kind of life these people actually lived. Here at this lakeside camp 9,000-year-old rolls of birch bark lay pickled in peat, waiting for their owners to repair the canoe, to make a basket or mend a leaky roof. These are the echoes of past lives which bring our distant ancestors into the present and make them accessible and real. Environmental archaeologists look at the pollen grains, snippets of charcoal and sediments and enable us to reconstruct a landscape in which birch and pine forests are dotted with lakes. Analysis of the animal bones and deer antlers shows us people living around a lake in the late spring and through the summer. The bones of a fish-eating dog say that the seaside was home at other times of the year. Experimental archaeologists, using replicas of the stone tools fill the camp with people busily cutting, scraping, piercing and whittling. A deer antler frontlet with two holes brings back to life a ritual in which humans travelled into the spirit realm in animal form or, more prosaically, a hunter disguised as a deer, waiting patiently for prey to pass by.

Life for Cheddar Man, his family and friends was probably very similar, differing in the details of the landscape, the timing of camp movements and perhaps styles of clothes and local dialect. Gough's Cave offers something else which is vital for bringing the Mesolithic to life, human bones. The skeleton of Cheddar Man is the most complete from this period in Britain and its analysis reveals much about the man and his times. Not only that, but modern forensic techniques allow us a peek at what the man himself may have looked like.

Putting flesh on the bones

The discovery of ancient DNA in Cheddar Man and the match made with Adrian Targett brought this important heap of bones back into the scientific limelight. The skeleton had been studied in 1914 and then again in 1937 after more bones were recovered from his original resting place. A thorough re-analysis using modern scientific methods had to wait until a television programme rediscovered this old star. The media and the public were keen to see how Adrian's ancestor looked and the reconstruction which followed produced unexpected insights into the personal life of Cheddar Man. Ever since its discovery the skull has excited speculation about death from a blow to the head. In 1998, a team of pathologists at Manchester University, led by Robert Stoddart, reported the results of their analysis.

The skull showed that several blows to the head had made Cheddar Man's life a misery and eventually killed him. A tiny piece of bone seems to have become lodged inside the skull as a result of a blow between the eyes. A large abscess formed, giving Cheddar Man a permanent headache and an odd appearance, not to mention probably a bad temper. The abscess could have killed him if it became infected and it probably did. He died at about the age of 40. We forget in our world awash with antibiotics just how lethal infections can be.

The Manchester team also reconstructed his face using techniques normally reserved for identifying murder victims. Strips of clay were laid layer by layer across the cheek bones, along the jaw, around the eyes and onto the skull to mimic the position and thickness of muscles. X-rays of the skull revealed a lopsided face, probably from childhood, which was broad with a rounded forehead (**81**). They also gave him a stubby nose, big watery eyes an unkempt head of hair and straggly moustache. This was no male model. Stoddart in speaking to the press observed that Cheddar Man was 'not particularly good looking. I suspect he looked like any modern inhabitant of a Somerset pub.' Perhaps a bit unfair to the people of Somerset but the meaning was clear, Cheddar Man was a fully modern human, however unprepossessing.

81   The face of Cheddar Man reconstructed by medical artist Denise Smith of Manchester University. To the left is Cheddar Man before being given a beard and straggly hair (photo: News Team International Ltd).

The end of the journey

This disfigured ancestor of living Europeans has been our guide to the evolution of humans, from the first faltering steps of a bipedal ape to settled farmers. His story is our story. It involves some of the great issues of modern archaeology: what makes us human, where and how did *Homo sapiens* evolve and why did we domesticate plants and animals? These are fundamental questions about ourselves as a species.

Five million years ago, in a world of forests, the first human ancestors emerged in Africa as adaptable two-legged apes able to feed on the ground or in trees and to walk between ever distant patches of food and shelter during daylight hours. These features became advantages as the earth cooled, dry seasons became longer, forests shrank and the world became an altogether tougher place in which to live. In this challenging environment, some bipeds gained an edge, they began to make and use flakes and cobbles of stone to open up a new option for making a living: eating meat. These were the early members of our genus *Homo*.

More than one species of early *Homo* vied for success on the grasslands and woodlands of tropical Africa. From one of these, about 2 million years ago, *Homo erectus* emerged as a large-brained, lanky, fire using, tool making, meat eating globe trotter. This was the first human species to move beyond Africa and the longest-lived, lasting 1.5 million years. *Homo erectus* was successful. Despite its limited use of language and small range of tools, this species was for its time the cleverest thing on the planet. Its descendant in Europe, *Homo heidelbergensis*, developed into Neanderthal, a species well adapted to the rigours of the ice ages. Meanwhile in Africa, as the Neanderthals unknowingly became a branch line, the descendants of *erectus* became our main-line direct ancestors, *Homo sapiens*.

How, why and even just when this happened in Africa are still questions to be resolved and the cause of not a little controversy. Even more controversial is the argument that African modern humans spread into Asia and later into Europe, where they were more successful at making a living than indigenous peoples, including the cold adapted Neanderthals. But the combined evidence of DNA, human bones and archaeology is persuasive. Now that Neanderthal DNA has been found and is very different from ours we can speak even more confidently of an African origin for modern humans. The last Neanderthals alive, just 30,000 years ago, were not evolving into us. Their bones were still those of another species.

Archaeology tells a story of modern humans arriving in glacial Europe equipped with new types of tools, complex social networks and with a mastery of symbols or art. These three behaviours lie at the root of our success as a wandering and pervasive species. Our ability to adapt rapidly to changing circumstances also led to the manipulation of a few key plants and animals at the end of the last ice age, a process which has fundamentally changed the world in which we live. Domestication has been a two-way process. We are now just as dependant on a handful of species for our survival as they were on us for their success. The consequences of farming have been profound. In 10,000 years we have been transformed from a nomadic species to one rooted to villages, towns and cities. Our numbers have grown dramatically and continue to do so. Agriculture can simply feed more people. But it was the success of gathering and hunting in the first place which led to domestication, an act of desperation in the face of mounting numbers and a fickle climate.

Farming spread rapidly from its birthplace, reaching the Mendips from the Middle East — a distance of 2,500 miles (4,000km) — in just 4,000 years. For a radically new way of making a living, that is rapid. Adrian Targett's link to Cheddar Man tells us that this spread was not a simple matter of successful farmers sweeping away all before them. The story is more complicated than that. Indigenous hunter-gatherers adopted and adapted parts of the package of domesticates to suit their needs. They actively promoted the spread of farming and herding. But there is a risk of giving too much credit to Mesolithic peoples. The DNA evidence, both nuclear and mitochondrial, confirms that pioneer farmers also arrived, entering Europe and settling along the fertile river valleys.

How many and what languages these people spoke is still a matter of controversy. The recovery of more ancient DNA should resolve the issue of numbers, but language is carried by people not genes. Cheddar Man probably spoke a tongue inherited from his Upper Palaeolithic forebears, perhaps something resembling the Basque language. But Adrian Targett with his Mesolithic roots speaks English, an Indo-European language. This mismatch tells us that links between language, culture and the movement of people are anything but straightforward.

The challenge of our inheritance

As a species we have had to adapt to the new world of towns and cities that we created. We can no longer rely on the bonds of kinship to settle disputes between neighbours. New ways of co-existing have had to be developed which enable large numbers of people to live closely together, people with very little in common except for the place they live. Our inheritance as an adaptable, innovative species has made the urban experiment a relative success so far. We have devised legal systems to replace the old kinship-based codes of behaviour, and judges sit in place of the clan elders. Police keep the peace where once small communities relied on the threat of shame and ostracism to maintain order. A complex infrastructure of utilities and transportation supplies us with the essentials of water, food, energy and removes our waste. These are the basics of modern urban life.

We also have inherited a propensity to create enemies. Our Upper Palaeolithic ancestors used symbols and rituals to build a sense of community, of belonging to a larger group than the immediate family. This co-operative spirit probably played a vital role in displacing Neanderthals and in coping with the rigours of ice age Europe. Co-operation can turn into competition, however, once a common threat is removed. The same skills used to create a sense of belonging can be applied equally well to distancing 'us' from 'them'. We are one species but members of competing groups at many different levels: nation, region, city, football team, neighbourhood, school, class and religion, to name a few.

Perhaps Cheddar Man's ultimately fatal bang on the head was part of that competitive legacy. The state of his immediate ancestors at Gough's Cave provides strong evidence for the rough and tumble defence of their patch. Their cut and smashed bones, including the scalped and dented 'fruit bowl' skull, tell a story which is more likely to be one of brutality rather than an act of ritual reverence or the mere satisfaction of hunger. The rapidly changing climate of the late ice age may have pushed these inhabitants to extremes of behaviour. In southern Scandinavia, the late Mesolithic cemeteries, with their excellent preservation, show clear evidence of warring at a time of a growing population. This kind of evidence is rare, competition between humans may always have been fierce, but the evidence rarely survives.

Is this then the legacy of evolution, to be constantly at loggerheads with one another? A legacy is something handed down, passed on. We can look at it, learn from it, and be aware of it but we do not have to accept it. The past does not determine the future. The future is in our hands, and though they may be bloody they are also the hands which build schools, hospitals and inspirational works of art, the product of our brains, not just of our genes.

This was a big, big story. It continues to rumble round the world more than a year later. Film crews from Australia, Japan, Europe, the United States have trekked to Cheddar to film Adrian and repeat the story for their viewers. It featured in the DK Chronicle of 1997, alongside Dolly the cloned sheep and the death of Diana, Princess of Wales. The advertisement for the American Guinness Book of World Records 1997 promised interviews with people of the year like Madeline Albright, the highest woman ever appointed to American public office, and Adrian Targett, Cheddar school-teacher. Discover magazine named Cheddar Man one of the top science stories of the year.

> I had merely acted as the go-between to arrange the filming of the Saxon Palace in the grounds of my school for the 'Time Traveller' programme, and had agreed on the spur of the moment to have a DNA sample taken, yet everyone wanted to talk to me! My first year as 'Cheddar Man' has been full of incident. The Richard and Judy Show with Bryan Sykes from Oxford, a live chat show in Holland. Journalists from all over the world have called and come to Cheddar to interview me. CNN have filmed me, and the National Geographic Film Unit. People with my family name wrote from everywhere; one had come across records of a Targett who was transported to Tasmania from Somerset for sheep stealing! Margaret Drabble visited, researching a novel about ancestry and heredity. And I came face to face with my ancestor — a head re-constructed from the skull by Manchester University. It was almost as great a shock as first learning about our relationship. I suppose the question I've been most often asked is, 'How did it feel to be told you're related to Cheddar Man?' Apart from my initial reaction, best described as 'overwhelmed', 'stunned' and 'astonished', I still find it an incredibly difficult question to answer. *Adrian Targett*

The story so far of Cheddar Man is one that begins and ends with show biz. He was unearthed in 1903 by workmen improving the show-cave originally uncovered by Richard Gough After the discovery an archaeologist was summoned pretty soon to the scene to authenticate the remains and add to their audience appeal. The Goughs were showmen, this was a show-cave, and attracting punters to view the exhibits was the name of their game. They were good at it. Here was another star attraction. The archaeologist, Mr H. St. George Gray, curator of the Taunton Museum dated the remains between the Palaeolithic and the Neolithic, which was quite accurate. The cave owners printed a post-card bearing a picture of the bones and an extract from the newspaper report of his comments for sale in their shop.

Cheddar Man's second life on earth was as a peep show for commercial gain.

Our television series was also devised to entertain and educate a local viewership — and to keep us in work. The motives are not vastly different, and the product is the same in both cases. Beneath the surface razzmatazz, and a slight air of tacky glamour, there are positive gains for science, for history, and for the public interest in every sense of the words.

> It is the role of the individual in history that has always fascinated and intrigued me. The role of the individual is certainly present in the Cheddar Man story. The link between him and me is about 300 generations. But in order to get from him to me each person in between had a vital part to play. Remove one of them and the link is broken: or more precisely, remove one of them and the rest would never have existed. The story of Cheddar Man shows us Man's tenacity in surviving and reproducing himself: it also shows us Man's transience and fragility.
>
> The story of Cheddar Man is also somewhat paradoxical. In order to survive as an individual, Cheddar Man needed to exist as part of an extended family which must have co-operated in order to have survived. In an era which increasingly seems to emphasize individualism, often at the expense of the well being of others, perhaps the way of life my ancestor lived 9,000 years ago points the way for survival for all of us in the next millennium.
> *Adrian Targett.*

Mick Aston's HTV series, 'The Time Traveller', of which *In search of Cheddar Man* became the flagship programme, secured the best viewing figures of any regional programming originating in the south west during 1997, taking almost fifty percent of the audience share and beating the national BBC Channels and Channel Four at their own game.

There is an insatiable demand for news of the past. We are still eagerly waiting for Bryan Sykes to unveil a longer DNA genealogy — possibly between the older Cheddar skeletons and one or more of the modern Cheddar residents from our sample. For Cheddar Man has still much to tell us — about himself, about ourselves, about the common genetic inheritance that unites our warring species, and that links all of us living today to common ancestors even older than Cheddar Man. It has been a privilege and it has been a pleasure to play a small part in uncovering a small part of that history.

Appendix: dating techniques

Technique	range (years)	materials dated
radiocarbon	historic to 40,000	charcoal, bone, other organics
K-Ar	35,000 to 1,000,000s	volcanic rocks
u-series	1,000 to 800,000	cave deposits, coral, teeth
TL	historic to 250,000	pottery, burnt rock, sediments
ESR	1,000s to 100,000s	tooth enamel, cave deposits

The dating techniques described here are based on the radioactive decay of unstable elements, or isotopes. The rate at which half the atoms of an isotope decay into another isotope is its **half-life**. Decay rates are constant and the half-lives are known, which gives the basis for creating a radioactive clock. The methods most commonly used to estimate the age of sites and artefacts are **radiocarbon dating, accelerator mass spectrometry** (AMS), **uranium-series** (u-series), **thermoluminescence** (TL), **electron spin resonance** (ESR) and **potassium-argon dating.** These techniques provide a date in years before present (BP), or 'absolute' dates. Older but still widely used techniques of 'relative' dating — such as changes in artefact styles in a stratigraphic sequence — are not discussed here.

Radiocarbon dating, the best known dating technique, is based on a half-life of 5,730 years for the isotope carbon-14 (^{14}C). After this length of time, only 50% of the original quantity of atoms of ^{14}C remain in a sample, after two half-lives or 11,460 years 25% remains, after three half-lives or 17,190 years just 12.5% remains and so on. After seven half-lives, or about 40,000 years, the amount of ^{14}C in a sample is too small to measure with confidence. Thus an age of 40,000 years is the practical working limit of radiocarbon dating.

All radioactive techniques involve a certain amount of statistical uncertainty when calculating an age, expressed by a + and - figure after the date, e.g., $1,000 \pm 100$ BP. This error range means that the sample has a 66% chance, or one standard deviation, of falling into the time range, e.g., 1,000 BP $\pm$ 100 BP = 1,100 to 900 BP. Two standard deviations will give a 95% probability of the age being correct.

Although radiocarbon dating is one of the most widely used techniques for dating the recent archaeological record, especially the Upper Palaeolithic and later periods, it has an inherent problem. Carbon-14 is produced in the upper atmosphere and enters the food chain as carbon dioxide through plants. All living things contain the current ratio of carbon-14 isotope to its sister isotopes of carbon-12 and carbon-13. When an organism dies, it stops taking up ¹⁴C from the environment and the isotope begins to decay at its half-life. We now know that the atmospheric ratio of carbon isotopes has not been constant in the past. Radiocarbon dates before 1,000 BC (3,000 years ago) are slightly too young so a correction factor or **calibration curve** derived from other dating techniques (such as tree-ring or uranium-series) is applied. Uncalibrated dates are not the equivalent of actual calendar years and are presented as dates BP, as in this book. Calibrated dates are presented as 'Cal BC/AD'.

Accelerator mass spectrometry (AMS) is a new measuring technique which counts directly the number of carbon atoms in a sample and should, in theory, extend the use of radiocarbon dating to samples older than 40,000 years. In practice, contamination of samples by other sources of carbon has caused problems. AMS dating has the great advantage of using only tiny amounts (5-10 milligrams) of an archaeological sample to produce a date. Precious artefacts such as the skeleton of Cheddar Man or cave paintings can now be dated directly with minimal damage.

In the 1980s, new dating techniques came to the aid of archaeologists interested in events older than 40,000 years — the working limit of radiocarbon dating. **Uranium-series** (u-series), **thermoluminescence** (TL) and **electron spin resonance** (ESR) fill an important gap between radiocarbon and **potassium-argon dating** (K-Ar).

K-Ar has a large half-life of 1,300 million years and is best used to date the decay of gases trapped in volcanic deposits older than 750,000 years. This technique has been crucial in establishing the evolution of early *Homo* in the volcanic regions of Africa and Asia where archaeological deposits are sandwiched between layers of ash. The technique is less useful for dating the evolution of the more recent archaic *Homo sapiens* and does not work outside areas of volcanism.

U-series, thermoluminescence and ESR dating techniques rely on the constant accumulation of the by-products of radioactive decay — electrons. These techniques count the number of electrons trapped in mineral crystals over time and assume a constant radiation dose from the surrounding environment. Some 'zeroing' event is needed to clear the mineral crystals of old electrons before the radioactive clock can work. This can be burning in a hearth or exposure to sunlight in the case of TL, the formation of the crystals in tooth enamel with ESR or the growth of calcium carbonate cave deposits for u-series dating.

Ideally, archaeologists like to apply more than one dating technique to a site or artefact, and to have a suite of consistent dates. A single date, even a radiocarbon date with a small error margin, is always a worry.

A final word of caution. Most dating techniques provide an age for the *context* or deposits associated with an artefact and do not date the artefact directly. AMS dating is an exception. Taphonomic processes (see Chapter 2) can mix artefacts and deposits of different ages and give misleading results. Careful excavation is a prerequisite for the application and interpretation of dating techniques.

Further reading

Aldhouse-Green, Stephen, Katharine Scott, Henry Schwarcz, Rainer Grün, Rupert Housley, Angela Rae, Richard Bevins, and Mark Redknap. 1995. Coygan Cave, Laugharne, South wales, a Mousterian site and hyaena den: a report on the University of Cambridge excavations. *Proceedings of the Prehistoric Society* 61: 37-79.

Andrews, Peter. 1990. *Owls, caves and fossils.* London: Natural History Museum Press.

Bahn, Paul, and Jean Vertut. 1997. *Journey through the Ice Age.* London: Weidenfeld & Nicolson.

Balch, H.E. 1947. *The Mendip caves.* Bristol: John Wright & Sons.

Barham, Lawrence. 1998. Possible early pigment use in the Middle Pleistocene of south-central Africa. *Current Anthropology* 39 (4).

Barton, Nicholas. 1997. *Stone Age Britain.* London: Batsford/English Heritage

Barton, Nicholas, Alison Roberts, and Derek Roe (eds). 1991. *The Late Glacial in north-west Europe: human adaptation and environmental change at the end of the Pleistocene.* Council for British Archaeology Report 77.

Bell, Martin, and Michael Walker. 1992. *Late Quaternary environmental change.* Harlow: Longman Group

Bonsall, Clive (ed). 1989. *The Mesolithic in Europe.* Edinburgh: John Donald.

Campbell, John. 1977. *The Upper Palaeolithic of Britain: A study of man and nature in the late Ice Age.* Oxford: Clarendon Press

Clark, J G D. 1954. *Excavations at Star Carr.* Cambridge: Cambridge University Press.

Cunliffe, Barry (ed). 1998. *Prehistoric Europe: an illustrated history.* Oxford: Oxford University Press.

Currant, Andy, Roger Jacobi and Chris Stringer. 1989. Excavations at Gough's cave, Somerset 1986-7. *Antiquity* 63: 131-6

Fagan, Brian. 1998 (9th ed). *People of the earth: An introduction to world prehistory.* New York: Harper Collins.

Gamble, Clive. 1986. *The Palaeolithic settlement of Europe.* Cambridge: Cambridge University Press.

Goudie, Andrew. 1992. *Environmental change.* (3rd ed). Oxford: Oxford University Press.

Green, Stephen, and Elizabeth Walker. 1991. *Ice Age hunters: Neanderthals and early modern hunters in Wales.* Cardiff: National Museum of Wales.

Jacobi, Roger. 1985. The history and literature of Pleistocene discoveries at Gough's Cave. *Proceedings of the University of Bristol Spelaeological Society* 17(2): 102-15

Jones, Steve, Robert Martin and David Pilbeam (eds). 1994. *The Cambridge Encyclopedia of human evolution.* Cambridge: Cambridge University Press.

Krings, Matthias, Anne Stone, Ralf Schmitz, Heike Krainitzki, Mark Stoneking and Svante Pääbo. 1997. Neanderthal DNA sequences and the origin of modern humans. *Cell* 90: 19-30.

Mellars, Paul. 1996. *The Neanderthal legacy.* Princeton University Press.

Pitts, Michael, and Mark Roberts. 1997. *Fairweather Eden: life in Britain half a million years as revealed by the excavations at Boxgrove.* London: Century.

Price, T Douglas, and Erik Petersen. 1987. A Mesolithic camp in Denmark. *Scientific American* 256: 90-9.

Proctor, CJ, and SN Colcutt, AP Currant, CJ Hawkes, DA Roe and PL Smart. 1996. A report on the excavations at Rhinoceros Hole, Wookey. *Proceedings of the University of Bristol Spelaeological Society* 20(3): 237-62.

Richards, Martin, Helena Côrte-Real, Peter Forster, Vincent Macaulay, Hilde Wilkinson-Herbots, Andrew Demaine, Surinda Papiha, Robert Hedges, Han-Jürgen Brandt, and Bryan Sykes. 1996. Paleolithic and Neolithic lineages in the European mitochondrial gene pool. *American Journal of Human Genetics* 59:185-203.

Roe, Derek. 1981. *The Lower and Middle Palaeolithic periods in Britain.* London: Routledge & Kegan Paul.

Schick, Kathy, and Nick Toth. 1993. *Making silent stones speak.* New York: Simon & Schuster.

Smith, Christopher. 1992. *Late Stone Age hunters of the British Isles.* London: Routledge.

Stringer, Chris. 1985. The hominid remains from Gough's Cave. *Proceedings of the University of Bristol Spelaeological Society* 17(2):145-52.

Stringer, Chris, and Clive Gamble. 1993. *In search of the Neanderthals.* London: Thames & Hudson.

Stringer, Chris, and Robin McKie. 1996. *African exodus: the origins of modern humanity.* London: Jonathan Cape.

Stuart, Anthony. 1988. *Life in the Ice Age.* Princes Risborough: Shire Books.

Waltham, AC, MJ Simms, AR Farrant, and HS Goldie. 1996. *Karst and caves of Great Britain.* London: Chapman & Hall.

White, Tim. 1992. *Prehistoric cannibalism at Mancos 5MTUMR-2346.* Princeton: Princeton University Press.

Whittle, Alasdair. 1996. *Europe in the Neolithic: the creation of new worlds.* Cambridge: Cambridge University Press.

Wymer, John. 1991. *Mesolithic Britain.* Princes Risborough: Shire Publications.

Index